The Mitchley Waltz

Raymond Stuart Canham

Photo credits. Most attributable to Iris Edgar, Norman Edgar,
Don Canham and Ray Canham. Others unknown.

ISBN: 9798734665077

DEDICATION

This is for Norman and Linda, with apologies for my absent years,
and for Pam, for steering the rest of the Tottenham family
with love and skill.

And also to Tina and Peter for being there.

CONTENTS

ACKNOWLEDGMENTS

Thank you to James, Matt, Juliet, Louise, Dominic, Izabela, and everyone who has helped pull this together.

My heartfelt thanks, love, and appreciation to Alison, who has put up with my tantrums, doubts and fears with commendable grace and good humour.

And to you, you gorgeous being, for buying this book.

Figure 1

Introduction

In July 2018 I was sitting at my mother's bedside in the Accident and Emergency department of Ipswich hospital. She was telling a young doctor that she was sorry for the inconvenience and hoped that she could do something for her legs while she was in, so that she could dance again.

Earlier that day I had, at her request, turned her front room that she had once used to teach dancing, into a downstairs bedroom. For the previous few months she had mostly slept downstairs in her chair. She could barely walk without a frame and even with one she struggled. Carers came in during the day, a situation that she tolerated if they made a fuss of her dog and fed him before they attended to her.

She had admired her new bedroom, tried the bed, and asked for a couple of things from upstairs to be brought down. A friend of hers had sorted her clothes and I had left her that night confident that she had everything she needed.

As soon as I was out of the door she had decided to go upstairs anyway. She fell, bounced off the sides on her way back down, and landed headfirst onto flagstones where she lay bleeding and unconscious. She may not have survived had she not landed on her emergency pendant and triggered the alarm, the emergency pendant that she only wore because everyone nagged her to. That, coupled with the quick thinking of her friend and first contact, saved her life.

Her health had been deteriorating to the point where some form of care home would soon become a necessity, but the general view was that it could be delayed because of the arrangements we had put in place.

Tackling the stairs was typical of her. She had been told by the district nurse, her doctor, her friends, and by me not to use them. But defiance of 'experts', especially medical ones, was a policy that had mostly served her well. As a 28-year-old tuberculosis survivor with one functioning lung she

1

had been told not to dance anymore, but she did anyway. As a 31-year-old new bride she was told not to have children, but a couple of years later out I popped.

When I was born in the early 1960s society was still quite conservative and traditional. Despite the 60s reputation for enlightenment, suburban England was a place of old-style values. My father was the breadwinner and went to the office Monday to Friday.

On Saturdays he mowed the lawn, and we might go out to a park or take the dog for an extra-long walk, as long as we were home in time for the football results. Some evenings were reserved for social activities, usually dances. On Sundays he went to church with the Boys Brigade where he was the band instructor, came home and washed the car, maybe did a little gardening or we might go for a drive.

My mother would have his dinner ready when he got home from work every night. She would do the laundry on Saturday afternoons after her morning dance class and Saturday evenings were often taken up with her leading a social dance somewhere. She never drove, relied on my father for housekeeping money and generally took a back seat to him.

Except when it came to dancing, where she was most certainly in charge.

As I grew up I could at times sense her resentment that dancing took second place to being a housewife, something to be squeezed into her 'free' time. Not that my father wasn't supportive. He drove her around, made himself scarce when necessary and in their own way they worked out a loving and mutually supportive balance between them.

With the benefit of hindsight, the suburban housewife role was not one that she was cut out for and secretly, maybe subconsciously, she knew it. It is a theme I will cover in more detail later.

She thought that me coming along stifled her independence and career as a dance teacher even more. We had a difficult relationship. She did not show affection with cuddles or physical closeness and she was not tactile or warm in a motherly way. Her plan was to pack me off to boarding school, a strategy she articulated on more than one occasion. Fortunately, for me at least, my father, not the world's most demonstrative man despite his 'head of the household' status, put his foot down. He had already been estranged from his daughter (from a previous marriage) since my mother came along, so he was not going to lose me.

But if this paints her in a poor light, let me add some balance. She wasn't abusive or unkind and I didn't want for much growing up. In many ways I was very fortunate.

I have many happy childhood memories, she was there when I needed her, she never laid a finger on me in anger (a dinner plate once, but that is another story) and she gave me a fierce and determined independence. She taught me a lot and she was not a bad person. Like all of us she was a product of her upbringing and experiences and as we will see, things were not always easy for her.

After my father died in 1986, she dusted herself off and took on the house they had shared in Suffolk, all five bedrooms and that narrow winding stairway and flagstone hall. Armed with her trusty dogs she carried on teaching and dancing with renewed vigour.

We became closer; I was a young man, she soon had grandchildren and we developed a way of expressing our affection without words or touching. I would lop trees in her garden, saunter around the garage with power tools, mend things for her and make a fuss of the dog. She would spend Christmas and new year with us, where she would cook a dinner, shower the grandchildren with affection and we would chat about nothing of any consequence.

After her fall she could not return home. Although the bruises healed, her mobility became even more restricted and she moved into a nursing home, initially as a temporary measure but it quickly became a permanent move.

It was during this time that I got to know her. After 50 or so years I began to understand the person who had, against medical advice, brought me into the world and raised me.

Her mind became more comfortable in the past and she would tell me and my wife things I had never known about her. Under gentle questioning I came to feel for her, to understand a bit more about how, through sheer bloody-minded determination, she had defied the odds and built a successful career as a dance teacher. She had juggled being a mother, wife and daughter, a much loved and admired instructor working with adults who have a learning disability and a generous and giving grandmother.

The first, and only time that I recollect we said that we loved each other was when she was on her death bed.

A few years later I found a diary that she had kept from 1958. Reading that, and then two others that came to light, has helped me understand her in a way I never managed to while she was alive. The diaries also offer a fascinating glimpse into the 1950s, and insight into a life confined to bed with TB, to ballroom dancing for pleasure and profit, to social activities and to the hopes and fears of the generation rebuilding Britain after the Second World War.

Figure 1 The author and his mother circa 1964.

Foreword

By Nicola & Jenny

Nicola and Jenny, former pupils of Iris's who I met up with again at her funeral.

'Iris taught us to dance when we were young, her enthusiasm and love of dancing instilled in us a lifetime love of dancing which we are still enjoying today.

We used to look so forward to the classes, which helped a lot with our confidence. Iris will always hold a special place in our hearts for developing our love of dancing.

We feel honoured to be asked to write this little contribution to the story of Iris's life.'

Nicola & Jenny
April 2021

.

Figure 2

Chapter 1
6^D Exercise Book

Reading someone else's diary is a risky enterprise. You are venturing into their private space, the place where thoughts and feelings, ideas and desires are recorded that otherwise would not, probably should not, see the light of day. We are all capable of flights of fancy in the privacy of our own heads, fantasies that we would never think of carrying out in real life or thoughts we dare not express anywhere but in our private journal.

While I was sorting out my mother's belongings after she moved into the nursing home, I put her diaries into a plastic box along with old photos and the other detritus accumulated throughout her life and dropped it into a storage unit. By then her eyesight had deteriorated to the point where reading them was not possible and space in her room was limited. I am not even sure if she knew that she still had them.

She died a few years later and I came to treasure those last few years as the closest I had really been to her.

It was while emptying the storage unit and sifting through her belongings that I found her diaries again. I couldn't get rid of them and I couldn't read them so into the loft they went.

A house move prompted more sorting of boxes and mostly vain attempts to compress as much as possible into as small a space as practical.

When I was balancing a box on my head while trying to get up a ladder and through the ridiculously small loft hatch, I looked down and saw a dull red notebook with loose pages, leaflets and other papers sticking out that I'd accidently left on the table below.

I decided it would have to stay where it was.

Twenty minutes later, with a grazed elbow and the remains of a dead mouse from the loft safely disposed of, I picked up the book.

It was a deep red Lion Brand Exercise Book that cost 6 old pence. I took out what turned out to be the programme for My Fair Lady at the Theatre Royal, Drury Lane. The programme gave me a glimpse into another world, a world within living memory for many, but different in so many ways; advertisements for Albany cigarettes, clothes 'of the moment' at Fenwicks of Bond Street, Murray's Cabaret Club, Morphy-Richards Floor-to-Ceiling Super-Suction Cleaner for only £24.19.0 inc. tax - complete with attachments, and last, and possibly least, North Thames Gas.

One piece of paper that I found tucked inside the diary matched one my father had kept in his Boys Brigade briefcase which was also stored in the loft. Both were small newspaper cuttings, the type of story one finds tucked away on page seven of the local newspaper, and they both covered the same item.

Tottenham's... *"own" Waltz - The Mitchley Waltz, music by Mr. D. Cannon (sic) ...dance steps in old tyme style ... by Miss Iris Edgar."*

It obviously meant a lot to them, their own dance, conceived, written, and performed by them in 1958, before they were officially a couple. I like to think that in some way their own Waltz helped bring them together.

It took me a long time to pluck up the courage to read the diary though. It felt intrusive, as if I were betraying her trust. I suppose that was exactly what I was doing. It was with a sense of curiosity mixed with fear that I opened a few random pages, initially to see what was there and if it was something to be kept or thrown away.

It was the artifacts, saved letters and programmes that finally pulled me in. Gradually the story started to evolve and grow into a narrative that I found entrancing, charming and at times surprising.

Over the following days I delved a little deeper.

Life in London in the late 50s started to be revealed, a world I had heard about and streets I recognised. Places I had visited and could conjure up memories of, were being populated with people I knew, and people I didn't know but had heard about.

As a child I always thought my parents' lives started when they got married. Or was it when I came along? Or three years later when the family upped sticks and moved out of London and into commuter belt Hertfordshire?

Slowly and surely, through reading the diary, I was drawn into a time before I was born, into years that saw significant changes, to England, to London and particularly to my parents and sister.

I discovered a world I thought I knew but realised that I had no understanding of, and I found the woman who had brought me into the world and raised me, but who was almost a stranger to me.

To begin to understand her I had to go back to the year when her life changed.

Or so I thought.

The first draft of this book was written on that assumption. While it was being edited, both Alison (my wife and editor) and I realised that something was missing. The story left a lot of questions unanswered.

Then fate intervened. Two more diaries came to light, 1955 and 1956, and along with them, joy of joys, photos, and other mementoes of those years.

A more complete picture was emerging, and the book was falling into place, albeit one that, despite some thorough searching, was missing any written record of 1957. Just a few photos of that year hint at what was happening but…well, you will find out soon enough.

1958 still features as the pivotal year in our story, the year it felt as if I was living in for most of 2020, but like any tale there is a back story that goes some way towards explaining why my parents became the people I knew.

The diary section of this book starts with selected highlights from 1955, then a more complete and more vivid 1956, before we immerse ourselves in 1958. The entries are mostly set in or around Tottenham, North London.

Before the diary I'll delve deeper into some themes that helped me navigate the world of my parents and the era in which they met.

Figure 2 Extract from 1958 diary

Figure 3

Chapter 2

Keep cheery

If you open the book 'Images of Cambridge'[1], one picture in the Cambridge at War chapter stands out. It is of a group of child evacuees from London filing out from the railway station. At the head of the group is a determined young girl with a pudding-basin haircut, what appears to be more luggage than anyone else and a challenging look towards the camera.

There is nothing pensive or frightened in her demeanour. You could be forgiven for thinking that being uprooted from her home in the middle of a war was something she was taking in her stride.

That was my mother.

Iris Olive Rose Canham, nee Edgar.

In a class picture taken to celebrate the coronation of George VI in 1937 the same look of steely eyed determination glares at the camera from beneath that familiar brutal haircut.

It is an unmistakable look. One that holds your attention, whether you want it to or not. Intelligent, wily and ever-so slightly sinister.

It is a look that says its owner takes no prisoners, yet may be amiable and beguiling if you take the time and effort to get to know her, so long as it's on her terms.

That was my mother.

---

[1] Cambridge Evening News, compiled by Michael J. Petty MBE.

In Cambridge she stayed with spinster sisters in their big house near the railway line. After just four months she moved back to London, along with her mother and baby brother, who had been evacuated to the village of Waterbeach, a few miles outside of Cambridge.

Back in Tottenham the family re-joined her father, George, who had a reserved occupation at an ironmongers, and who led the local Fire Wardens in true Dads Army style, equipped with a colander 'borrowed' from work for head protection.

Two days after she moved back, the house in Cambridge she had been staying in was badly damaged by a bomb intended for the nearby railway yard.

'I suppose no one had told Hitler I'd moved back to London' she said later when asked about it.

That was my mother.

The following year, 1940, the war reached the home front in earnest. Bombing raids on London were a regular occurrence and on 7th September 1940 London was bombed for 57 consecutive nights, accounting for around 40,000 civilian deaths during 'The Blitz'.

Along with many families the Edgars took refuge in their Anderson Shelter, built by George in the back garden of 14 Dorset Road, while they listened to the drone of wave after wave of aeroplanes overhead.

'Maybe Hitler had found out I was back in town', she'd tell us.

Back in her familiar stomping ground, Iris spent the rest of the war watching the sky for 'doodle bugs' and enemy bombers, scavenging on bomb sites and helping her mother the dress maker, who had trouble keeping up with orders for hastily arranged weddings and funerals.

At Downhills Central School she rose quickly from near the foot of the class table at the end of 1941, with a poor attendance record, to 'a steady and conscientious worker' and 'a good reliable prefect' with 100% attendance in 1945.

By then she excelled at the subjects that she had decided she needed for work, English, Shorthand and Bookkeeping, and less so at others, like Algebra, which she had decided she didn't need and therefore took no interest in

That was my mother.

Aa a young adult there were two things that came to dominate her life above everything else.

The first deprived her of those free and easy years between a childhood overshadowed by the war, and the responsibilities of marriage. The time when the world is your oyster and anything and everything seems possible.

Tuberculosis (TB) made sure she spent those years in a state of inertia, 'on-hold' as it were, until she could re-join the rest of the world and try and catch up.

Many in her position grew old before their time. They spent years convalescing in dressing gowns and slippers, too weary and defeated to bother with anything but the daily routine of bed rest and deliberately unexciting pastimes sanctioned by the consultants and Matron.

It was perhaps the second thing that dominated her life that prevented her from lapsing into early middle age.

Ballroom dancing.

Her love, her gift and, as we will see, her salvation.

That was my mother.

To get an idea of the woman who sat in her draughty bedroom in a small house on a lonely back street of Tottenham, working towards her dream of being a professional dance instructor, we need to first understand some of the factors that helped mould her.

Firstly, a disease that accounted for one in every four deaths in 18th century England, and that claimed the lives of Robert Louis Stevenson, John Keats, the Bronte sisters, Eleanor Roosevelt, George Orwell, Jane Austen, Pocahontas, King Edward VI and Franz Kafka, among millions of others over centuries - Tuberculosis.

Figure 3 Iris 1933

Figure 4

Chapter 3
Shouting and whistling are forbidden

Dancing has many health benefits, including promoting a strong heart and lungs, increased muscular strength, endurance and aerobic fitness, maintaining muscle tone, increased strength, and strong bones.

To be a dancer requires stamina, coordination, and a reasonable level of fitness.

So, when the comparatively gentle exertion required to learn a new waltz started to leave Iris breathless it was obvious that something was not right. Being stolid and independent by nature she ignored it.

A routine x-ray screening at work in 1955 revealed a tell-tale shadow on her lung and she was confined to bed at home and supervised by the TB clinic at nearby St. Ann's hospital.

She spent much of 1955 at home in bed, gradually increasing her activity until, in early 1956 she was considered well enough for fresh clean air and plenty of exercise.

That was to be a brief interlude away from the grip of bed rest and hospitals though.

I'd heard of TB of course, and understood that my mother had suffered from it, but I never really knew any details.

TB is a disease caused by bacteria called Mycobacterium tuberculosis. It is highly infectious, and anyone can catch it by breathing in the tuberculosis bacteria. Most people's immune system either kills the bacteria or keeps it under control and they will be symptom free and probably not even aware that they have it.

For some people though, their system does not suppress the bacteria and they become ill, often weeks or even years after the initial infection. Between five and ten people out of 100 with latent TB in their body can become ill later if the bacteria multiply.

Infection leading to illness is associated with a variety of factors, including a compromised immune system, conditions like diabetes or unsanitary conditions. Overcrowding and proximity to infected people greatly increases the chances of someone catching it.

Although it can attack any part of the body tuberculosis of the lungs, Pulmonary TB, is the most common form. A person with Pulmonary TB will typically have laboured breathing, will cough up blood and become feverish. The blood becomes starved of oxygen and the person loses weight, will become pale and listless and may experience other complications such as a collapsed lung. In later stages of the disease depression often alternates with a state of euphoria called spes phthisica.

The onset and regression of Pulmonary TB could be menacingly slow, and the patient would appear to be 'consumed' by the disease, hence it often went by the name Consumption.

There is evidence of Neolithic skeletons having TB, but it does not appear to have become endemic until the 17th century and really took off with the industrial revolution and the urbanisation and poor sanitation that came along with it.

Because of its association with the arts through poets like Keats and pre-Raphaelite art such as John Everett Millais's painting Ophilia, featuring 'consumptive' model Elizabeth Siddal, symptoms such as depression and euphoria were viewed as evidence of a creative soul that raised the mind to a higher state of artistic consciousness. Consequently, in the mid-1800s a fashion developed for the 'consumptive look' and otherwise healthy women starved themselves and whitened their skin with chemicals.

The First World War introduced the widespread use of chest x-rays for new recruits coupled with bacterial tests to distinguish between latent and active cases where the x-rays had showed up a tell-tale black spot on the lungs.

World War I also launched the use of cheap, widespread antibiotics which could suppress, but not cure, the disease. The only real cure at the time was rest, a healthy diet, gentle exercise, and plenty of time to recover, two years of rest and recuperation was not uncommon. Usually, a patient would be prescribed bed rest at home and if they did not improve, hospitalisation.

Before the introduction of the National Health Service in 1948, wealthy patients could choose to get out of polluted, overcrowded cities and convalesce in 'sanatoriums' in the countryside, where plenty of fresh air was believed to aid recovery from the disease. In their heyday 'sanatoriums' were at the forefront of all sorts of treatments, from 24-hour complete bed rest on verandas open to the elements, to experimental surgery, macabre machines that would collapse lungs to 'rest' them and all sorts of drug therapies of varying effectiveness and side effects.

In 1948 however most of the sanatoriums were absorbed into the NHS as convalescent homes and became the standard treatment method for TB patients not requiring hospital care.

Practices such as deliberate lung collapsing became less fashionable as drug therapies advanced and in 1955 a combination of three drugs, streptomycin, para-aminosalicylic acid and isoniazid was recognised as the most effective treatment.

Gradually drug treatment became more refined, and today TB can usually be treated effectively by antibiotics, but therapy is still a cocktail of drugs for up to 18 months, or more for drug-resistant TB.

St. Ann's General Hospital, in Tottenham, North London was to play a significant part in Iris' treatment for tuberculosis.

First opened in 1892 as London's North Eastern Fever Hospital and renamed in 1951, St. Ann's had 756 NHS beds and specialised in patients with chest disorders and infectious diseases.

When she was admitted, Iris was given a copy of *'Notes for the guidance of patients admitted to the chest unit'*, written in 1955 by T.A.C McQuiston M.D., Ch. B., Consultant Physician to the Chest Unit. This typed booklet gives an insight into the nature of TB treatment in the 1950s, particularly 'Grades' which are referred to in her diaries.

Dr. McQuiston wrote with a gruff, no nonsense style. You can practically smell the tweed and pipe smoke as you read his words. Here are a few highlights:

'If you feel you cannot adapt yourself to what in reality is a new and restricted way of life for many of you it is better to say so at the beginning and ask for your discharge…

Grades
These are the gradual steps by which you are returned to health and although they may seem irksome and trivial to some it must be realised that years of experience in the care of tuberculosis have gone into their formation and that breaking of a grade is tantamount to refusing treatment and the offender will be liable to instant dismissal.

Bed absolute - The patient does nothing for himself. He is fed, washed and bathed by the nursing staff.

B.1. Patient may feed himself but everything else is done for him.

B.2a Patient may wash and feed himself.

B.2b Patient may wash, feed and bath himself in bed.'

And so on…

'Smoking

It would be preferable if the patient could stop smoking altogether. However, it is realised that smoking in moderation is a comfort to those who enjoy it and it is therefore allowed at the following times...'

There then follow sections on visiting hours, rest hours, entertainment, and occupational therapy, all written in the familiar unequivocal style of Dr. McQuiston.

The final two paragraphs read:

"When living a communal life such as in a hospital ward it is necessary to give a little thought to the welfare of your fellow patients. Patients should therefore conduct themselves in a quiet and orderly manner. Shouting and whistling are forbidden and the use of obscene language will not be tolerated under any circumstances and patients using same will be asked to leave. Spitting is dangerous and will only be done into the cartons provided. Since tuberculosis is spread by dissemination of drops of moisture containing the germ never cough unless the mouth is covered with a handkerchief. Try and make this habit automatic. It will protect your family and friends. Windows will not be interfered with except with Sister's permission. Keep the grounds tidy. Don't throw rubbish out of the window and remember bread thrown to birds will also encourage rats and other vermin. If you have any complaints these should be discussed with a senior member of the hospital staff.

Having read the above rules and regulations you will no doubt be wondering what sort of prison you have been admitted to, but please remember they are for your own benefit and their obedience will considerably aid your recovery. You are not forced to obey: you can leave. Tuberculosis is a curable disease but it requires your absolute co-operation in order to get back to a normal life again."

The grades, which went from complete bed rest to being up and about for up to 4 hours, were applicable not just in hospital but also if you were prescribed best rest at home.

Iris' long battle with TB was over four years and its after-effects would haunt her for the rest of her life. She was under close supervision by the clinic at St Ann's both before hospitalisation and after being formally discharged in 1957.

She had been forbidden to dance again until given the all-clear by her consultant, which was unlikely to happen since TB had left her with only one functioning lung.

But dancing was her life, so she chose to carry on dancing anyway.

Figure 4 TB appointment letter 1956.

Figure 5

Chapter 4
Old Time Dancing

Dancing was how my mother defined herself, and how others knew her.

She may have been variously a daughter, sister, wife, stepmother, mother, widow, grandmother, friend, patient, secretary, personal assistant, artist, pianist, Christian, drama teacher, dance instructor, reader, gardener, dog lover and carer; she may also have had a distinguished career working with adults who have a learning disability, and she could cook a mean Christmas dinner, but first and foremost, she was a dancer.

Ballroom, Latin, Scottish, Country, Tap…dance ran through her veins. When she stepped onto the dancefloor with the poise that came naturally to her, she made the most complicated routine look easy in the way only the absolute best can do.

Teaching others to dance was her forte though.

Behind the microphone in front of a crowded hall or one-to-one in our front room with the special wooden floor, she was in charge and took no prisoners.

She expected the best from herself and no less from every student she ever taught, from the four-year-old in her big sister's old shoes and her teddy bear left on the chair, to the gold medal competition couple; from the adult ballroom dance display team on the village green to the adults with a learning disability performing on the London stage, she expected, demanded, and got, the best.

I do not know where her love of dancing came from, but my earliest memories of her revolved around music and dance.

She would host classes and private lessons in our front room in Sawbridgeworth. It was a four-bed semi built in the mid-1960s that my parents bought 'off-plan' and they managed to get a wooden floor installed in the lounge for mum's lessons.

I was a toddler when we moved there, and I grew up to the sound of strict-tempo dance music being played through her record player's crude amplifier at maximum volume, accompanied by her shouted instructions and remonstrations.

She would frequently lose her voice for days, sometimes weeks on end, but she carried on in a kind of barked whisper that nevertheless was still louder than the music. Her approach as a teacher seemed to be to intimidate every pupil until their inner dancer surrendered any resistance to the rhythm.

Sometimes she would play marching tunes on the piano for me and I'd stomp around the house; out of the living room, past the stairs and along the hall with the strange black and red swirled carpet, through the kitchen where my father taught me to play chess, then into the dining room with the sideboard carefully stacked with the best china and family hand-me-down tableware that I was forbidden to touch, and back into the lounge where I would be encouraged to do 'one more lap'.

Occasionally she would add in a waltz or quickstep and show me some of the steps. Only later in life did I come to realise that I was being taught to dance by stealth.

Gradually my involvement in dancing, like my sister's before me, would be more formal, if not entirely voluntary.

We both remember standing at our bedroom windows counting the girls (it was always girls) coming down the drive on a Saturday morning. An odd number meant that we would be roped in to make up the final pair.

As I got older, I protested but she just could not understand why anyone would not want to dance or why I was objecting when I knew what I was doing and was therefore of value to her.

So, I learnt to dance.

I was probably the only boy at Mandeville Junior School in Sawbridgeworth who knew his Foxtrot from his Gay Gordon. Indisputably I was the only boy who would be privy to that information for as long as I could trust the gaggle of Saturday morning girls to keep quiet about my involvement. Which they did because to be seen with, let along hold, a boy was tantamount to a gross betrayal of their gender in the politics of the school playground.

Looking back, I always thought of my mother as full of confidence on the dancefloor, but her diaries reveal her younger self to be less sure of her talents, even though she regarded her dancing as a gift.

Dancing was in her DNA, but then in the forties and fifties she was surrounded by it.

It is easy to underestimate the importance of dance halls on our culture. Formal Victorian sequence dances held under chandeliers in stately homes and up-market hotels attracted those with the means to dress formally and follow polite but rigid customs. Everyone else could attend casual dances in municipal buildings and church halls where they could frolic away with abandon.

In the early 20th century, class barriers became less rigid and popular social dancing developed into more relaxed occasions as the two styles merged. At the same time a trend grew in seaside holiday resort pavilions for dancing as entertainment, and pub landlords saw an opportunity to attract customers by providing floor space for dancing.

Dancing as a recreational activity, and of course as a popular and socially acceptable form of courtship, started to gain popularity and purpose-built dance halls started springing up to cater for the growing demand.

One of the most enduring, and iconic examples is the Tower Ballroom in Blackpool which was opened in 1899.

Up to the First World War many of the dance halls prospered as the working class were starting to have disposable income and leisure time.

After the war, entrepreneurs began repurposing and converting buildings into entertainment venues, seeing the potential to cash in on dance 'crazes' like ragtime, jazz and swing which kept punters interested as the fashions changed.

Attendance at dances understandably dipped during the Second World War, but they were still a popular recreation and meeting point both for troops on leave and forces stationed here from abroad, most notably Americans, who introduced new music and dances.

When the war ended dancing quickly regained its ground, to the extent that it was estimated that admissions to dances was around 200 million by 1953, double that of pre-war 1938.

There were between 400 and 500 new dance venues opened every year between 1920 and 1960, according to evaluations taken from local licensing authorities.

Social attitudes were changing and influences from Hollywood, none more so than Fred Astaire and Ginger Rodgers, were driving changes on the dancefloor too.

Dance classes became an integral part of society. People could learn the dances before trying out what they had learned on a night out. The big ballrooms usually had a live band, often as much a part of the entertainment as the dancing itself.

Late night London was made up of...

'Spindly tendrils, invisible to the untutored eye but familiar enough to musicians as the pathways to drill halls and club rooms and town halls and ballrooms and church halls and banqueting rooms where there took place every Saturday and Sunday night round the year, hundreds of homely social events...at eleven o'clock, having mangled the two obligatory last waltzes...the hired hand would spill out into the lamplit streets and sprint for the 11.14, perhaps hoping to find themselves sitting facing other musicians across the aisle of that swaying, racketing, somehow vaguely festive last train...' to quote from Swingtime in Tottenham by dance hall saxophonist Benny Green.

Meanwhile, thanks to technical innovations during World War 2, CBS-Columbia developed a 33.3 revolutions per minute (RPM) 12inch record with microgrooves, pressed onto vinylite (vinyl) which went on the market in 1948. The following year RCA Victor pressed the first 45 RPM 7inch records.

For dance teachers the advent of the portable record player, together with louder speakers and stronger, lighter records (the old 78 discs were very heavy and brittle) meant that they could hire, or be hired by, small halls and groups. Often these classes were as much a social occasion as going to the ballroom.

As styles and fashions changed, ballroom dancing retained its identity as a pastime that could be enjoyed by both children and adults with minimal instruction, by enthusiasts in clubs and by professionals on the dance circuit.

Where formal sequence dancing had largely depended upon couples moving together, some dances, like the waltz, started to introduce variants, where couples moved independently of each other within the framework of the dance.

This became modern ballroom and the foundation for formal dances and competitions, which featured selections from 'the big ten' dances; Waltz, Viennese Waltz, Tango, Foxtrot and Quickstep, and five Latin dances – Cha-cha-cha, Samba, Rumba, Paso Doble and Jive.[2]

For enthusiasts, ballroom dancing became known as Old Time (sometimes Tyme) Dancing, to distinguish it from the 'modern' styles like jazz and tap.

Such was ballroom dancing's popularity in the 50s that in 1958 the Royal Variety Performance featured a segment called 'Dancing Time' with The George Carden Dancers, The Dior Dancers, The Mecca Formation Dancers and Victor Silvester and his Ballroom Orchestra.

---

[2] The USA and Canada has slightly different classifications.

In Tottenham, North London, far away from the bright lights of the London Coliseum and its stars of stage, screen, and ballroom, Iris Edgar and Donald Canham were developing their very own dance, the Mitchley Waltz.

After being awarded a 'commended' Silver medal for Ballroom in 1957, by 1958 Iris was running a dance class in Tottenham, as well as taking lessons of her own with the aim of becoming an accredited dance teacher.

She was also holding down a full-time job and helping to keep her household together after her father left to move in with his mistress round the corner from the family home.

If TB had not stopped her ambitions to become a professional dance teacher though, there was always the possibility that becoming a housewife and mother might…

Figure 5 Iris, New Year Eve 1955.

Figure 6

Chapter 5
A woman's place

There was an emerging tension for women in the mid-1950s which resonated in my parents' world too.

Many people still expected a woman to be first and foremost a wife and mother. Gender roles were stereotypically divided into male and female responsibilities and were reinforced in popular media, in children's books, education and in the workplace.

The surge in consumer technologies like washing machines and vacuum cleaners gave the, ahem, 'bored housewife' time to peruse magazines aimed squarely at her.

In 1957 'Woman' magazine was read by an estimated 50% of the adult female population of the UK, and between 1957 and 1967 annual spending on weekly and monthly magazines peaked at £80 million a year.

These publications typically contained adverts that reinforced the housewife's life of domestic servitude. Take the 1958 advertisement from Hoover for example, that marketed their latest domestic appliance with the slogan,

"Christmas morning she'll be happier with a Hoover" alongside a picture of a presumably delighted housewife reading the instructions beside a gleaming Hoover vacuum cleaner. Unless she was reading a pamphlet about how to kill your thoughtless lump of a husband of course.

In the world of children's books, the popular Janet and John series taught a generation to read accompanied by Janet helping mum with the housework or in the kitchen while John cleaned the car with dad.

Dad went to work, mum stayed at home. Everyone looked happy with their place and the world of ruddy faced butchers (all men) and glamourous nurses (all women) ticked over like a well-oiled machine. Jane did not want to be a doctor or mechanic and John was destined to take up medicine, smoke a pipe and fix the car.

In education women were still pushed towards domestic subjects training them to become a housewife and mother. In 1954 a law was passed to limit the number of girls who could go to grammar school as it was considered that too many were passing the 11-plus examination and therefore keeping the boys out.

In 1959 the Crowther Education Report on education, commissioned by the government, postulated that, *"The prospect of courtship and marriage should rightly influence the education of the adolescent girl."*

Oh, and until the mid-1980s you were twice as likely to get into university if you happened to be born with a penis.

Meanwhile at work, equal pay was still a long way off for women.

Discrimination was only prohibited in 1975, with the introduction of the Sex Discrimination Act, which made it illegal to discriminate against women in work, education, and training. In the same year, the Employment Protection Act brought in statutory maternity provision. Suddenly a lot of bosses found that it was illegal to sack a woman because she was pregnant.

Even then it took many more years to get anything like proper parity. Hoover, to return to the world of domestic appliances for a moment, still had a 'women out first' redundancy policy in 1980. It was only challenged when women at their Merthyr Tydfil plant went on strike over it.

Also, in 1980, a woman could at last apply for credit in her own name for the first time - a year after Margaret Thatcher became the UK's first female Prime Minister.

'Traditional' gender roles may have been expected in the 1950s, but the challenges to them were slowly growing.

The reliance on men to go off and do the fighting during the Second World War had led to women increasing their presence in the workplace in non-traditional roles, such as engineers, bus drivers and skilled factory jobs, among many other positions formally the preserve of the menfolk.

Women's presence in these roles continued into peace time for a while, but as the casualties of war (understandably mostly male as they had gone off to fight) were replaced by the post war baby boomers - disproportionately male[3], their place in the workforce was generally

---

[3] More men tend to be born after wars. This is possibly associated with, how do I put this politely, rigorous sexual activity…because baby boys are more likely to be born to younger parents, and to those who conceive quickly. Young men returning as 'heroes' could be relied upon to fulfil these criteria. There is also the Travers-Willard evolutionary theory which postulates that a baby's gender will tend,

replaced by men.

Women, if they went to work, were often expected to leave when they got married. Frequently they were 'let go', in other words, sacked, because their place was now at home to look after their new husband and breed the next generation.

Iris was an elegant, articulate, and eligible lady who was expected, and probably expected of herself, to get married, settle down and have children; to play the dutiful wife.

She was also ambitious with a promising dancing career ahead of her. She took elocution lessons and voice training to be able to call-out instructions over records when instructing pupils.

Growing up in post war England, in a working-class part of North London with largely traditional values she must have been in a dilemma. It undoubtably caused her some internal debate, as her diaries reveal.

As a child I often visited Tottenham, and still know it quite well, but after reading the diaries I wanted to find out more about what it was like being brought up in this part of the rapidly expanding London suburbs of the 1950s.

Figure 6 Don, Iris and Raymond, circa 1964.

---

albeit marginally, towards the one favoured by maternal circumstances, and that boys therefore will do better in a society short of males, e.g. after a war.

Figure 7

Chapter 6
Toteham to Tottenham

Tottenham is believed to have been named after Tota, a farmer in the area, whose hamlet was mentioned in the Domesday Book as Toteham, from 'Tota's hamlet'.

It began as several distinct villages which gradually merged around the major thoroughfare of the A10, Old North Road and then spread out by filling the gaps, slowly but surely with housing.

Before the Second World War the area was a mixture of working-class families employed in the local factories, and middle-class commuters attracted by relatively low house prices. After the war, a lot of these houses were converted into flats and bedsits.

An influx of Irish and Greek Cypriot immigrants brought a different feel to parts of the borough, and Turkish Cypriots followed to work in the flourishing garment industry.

In the 1950s, like most London boroughs, Tottenham was a self-contained district with schools, places of worship, shops, a local football club, municipal parks and recreation facilities such as cinemas and dancehalls.

By the late 1950s things were changing as younger people moved into the area, attracted by flats and houses that were cheaper to rent than those closer to the city. The underground, over ground trains and bus routes provided good links into the centre of London.

Although largely residential, some local businesses and factories provided employment and supplied some familiar household names to the rest of the UK and abroad.

Basildon Bond stationery was produced locally by John Dickinsons, and nearby The Eagle Pencil Company produced the pencils, pens and erasers to write on it with.

Maynards made their famous Wine Gums here and Jamesons produced Raspberry Ruffles and Dairy Maid toffee among their various sweets and confectionery. Wonderloaf, which was once one of the most popular brands of sliced bread in the UK was produced in Tottenham too.

The Stencil Duplicator, forerunner of the office photocopier was manufactured by Gestetners in Broad Lane. Kolok Manufacturing produced carbon paper and print rollers and Lorilleux & Bolton produced ink for the printing trade.

Harris Lebus was a major furniture manufacturer who, during the Second World War, also built wooden airframes for Mosquito fighter planes, gliders used in the D-Day landings and wooden replica tanks.

Duncan Tuckers operated a large timber supply company and Challens made pianos, including, in 1935, the 'Largest Piano in the World' which was over 11ft long. It had a lengthy career in the under-appreciated world of oversized novelty keyboards but was recently re-discovered languishing in a barn in France. It arrived back in England in December 2020 and is being lovingly restored.

Blackmans mechanical engineers, Cannon Rubber, William Press engineering, Spong and Co. kitchen utensils, Barber's foundry and finishing shop and Sparklets - soda syphon canister makers were just some of the businesses local to Tottenham, as was Althorns of Clyde Circus where Iris' father worked.

Maybe it was an optimism born of this manufacturing base that led to its resurgence, but by the late 1950s Tottenham was a thriving area with a mixed community, busy shops and a vibrant night life.

At its core though, it remained staunchly blue collar, with many families having roots that spanned generations, all quietly going about their business behind the curtains of houses lining the miles of residential streets.

One of those streets, an anonymous cul-de-sac leading to a cement works, was Dorset Road. It took its name from the 17th Century owner of Tottenham Manor, the Earl of Dorset.

It is where our story will start, so let's meet some of the main characters.

Figure 7 Outside 14 Dorset Road, Norman right of picture.

26

Figure 8

Chapter 7
The Cast

Starring

Miss Iris Olive Rose Edgar – 25 years old in 1955, single. Works as an administrator for Middlesex Education Authority in central London. Lives with her mother and brother at 14 Dorset Road, Tottenham. Ballroom dance enthusiast, learning to be a dance instructor.

Mable Edgar - Iris and Norman's mother, recently divorced from their father. Dressmaker. Long standing member of the Civil Defence Corps and Women's Royal Voluntary Service. Lives at 14 Dorset Road.

Mr Donald (Don) Alfred Canham – Aka, Mr. Cannon - Accounts Clerk for British Petroleum (BP). Boys Brigade band instructor. Ex-Navy. Widowed when his first wife died following complications after childbirth. Father to Linda. Has just started taking dancing lessons with Miss Edgar.

Linda Canham - Daughter of Don Canham. Member of Miss Edgar's junior dance classes.

Norman Edgar - Iris's younger brother. Lives at 14 Dorset Road.

Special Guests

Jean (Canham) - The youngest of Don's brothers and sisters.
Pamela (Pam) Canham – Don's younger sister.
Gerry - Pam's fiancé.

Pete Canham – Don's younger brother.

Mr and Mrs Canham - Don's mother and father.

Supporting Cast

Mr and Mrs Foster – Owners of Leconfield Guest House – Isle of Wight.

Bernard – A gentleman acquaintance with intentions. Also, a guest at Leconfield.

John and Dorothy (Dot) – Guests at Leconfield.

Tony – A guest at Leconfield. *'A most ferocious liar with x-ray eyes'*.

Ron & Kit – Guests at Leconfield.

Mary Kielthy - Shared a hospital ward with Iris, named witness in the bicycle clip scandal of 1956.

Father John D. Harrington – Assistant Curate St. Johns Vinery Church and Roman Catholic Padre to St. Ann's Hospital, Tottenham.

Mr J.R. Lloyd - Sub-Divisional Civil Defence Officer – Tottenham Sub-Division. Based at Tottenham Civil Defence Headquarters, Mitchley Road, N17.

Jean Elliott– Manageress of record shop. Went out with someone famous – guitar playing friend of Iris and member of the same art group.

Laurie Hookins – A member of Iris' dance classes. *'A strange fellow'*.

Betty - Betty Dyce - Iris' dance instructor and lifelong friend.

The Stones – Mr & Mrs Stone. Don's father and mother-in-law. Grandparents to Linda

Tony Fisher - Trumpet player and a bit of a lothario.

George Charles Edgar - Mable's ex, father to Iris and Norman.

Introducing

Penny -The family dog. A standard poodle. A few years before the events in these diaries took place Iris took Penny on a walk one night and the dog stopped outside a house in a nearby street. This wasn't a one off, so curious to see why Penny was so familiar, she knocked on the door. Her father was inside with 'another woman'.

Luigi - the family budgie.

Not Appearing

Walter Canham – Don's eldest brother who was killed in World War 2 onboard HMS Penelope.

Butch – The family cat, who makes it into a few of Iris' photos but never gets a mention in her diaries.

Figure 8 George, Iris and Mabel.

Figure 9

Chapter 8
Diary notes

As I transcribed the diaries and Iris' story appeared, I noticed my computer was merrily flagging grammatical inconsistencies and errors at regular intervals. I decided to ignore the dictates of Microsoft and stick to as accurate a transcription as I could of my mother's writing.

Therefore, in the diary sections I have ignored modern conventions, like dropping the full stop after Mr. for example, and stuck rigidly to her spellings, grammar, and linguistic quirks. I hope by this I have been faithful to her 'voice'.

I have reproduced every single entry for 1956 and 1958 and selected entries for 1955. I wanted to demonstrate something of everyday life in 1956 for someone with TB and in 1958, to give a glimpse into a more normal life in North London, such as the gossip, reports of trips to the theatre and falling, or not, in love.

Several narrative strands started to emerge and flow through the years, as you will see.

Where days or in some cases whole months are missing that is because there were no entries at all. I do not know why and frustrating though it may be, I never will.

I wrestled with how to interpret and explain external events mentioned in her diary and have settled on footnotes. My intention is to add context to her story without disrupting the narrative. I hope that they do not become too intrusive.

On the topic of footnotes, these, along with some of the background material, relies on my research. I am not an academic, for example my computer just told me I'd spelled academic incorrectly, but what you'll read, I believe to be accurate, certainly enough to give a flavour of the topics in question.

If you notice any errors or inconsistencies, I take full responsibility. If you let me know I will do my best to update future copies.

Finally, when I re-read the manuscript, I noticed that I had changed how I referred to my mother, depending upon when I was writing. She was variously mother, mum or Iris. For consistency I have tried to keep it as Iris for most of the text, except for when I am referring to her in a personal way.

I'm sure it'll all make sense once you get started.

Figure 9 Butch, 1959.

1955

'I suppose this is all an experience!'

The Mitchley Waltz

Figure 10

Chapter 9
An Introduction to 1955

The United Kingdom celebrated the arrival of a new year with the formation of its very own RAF Squadron of atomic bombers on the 1st. of January 1955, heralding the start of the modern nuclear era.

Cinema goers could avoid pondering global annihilation by contemplating the ills of revolutionary communism and going to watch the first full-length British-made animation to be shown in cinemas, the never cheery adaptation of George Orwell's Animal Farm.

It was a bad year to travel by train it seemed, with three notable crashes. Accidents at Sutton Coalfield, Milton and Barnes accounted for 41 fatalities and 235 injuries between them.

Mind you, it was still safer than watching the Le Mans 24-hour race in France, where one single crash claimed at least 84 lives, 83 of them spectators. Later in the year, actor, pin up and auto-racing enthusiast James Dean was killed in a car crash in Cholame, California.

In April, ten years after steering the country through World War 2 and one year after the end of rationing, Winston Churchill resigned as Prime Minister.

Anthony Eden took his place, cementing his position the following month by winning a general election with a 31-seat majority.

The BBC had some competition when the Independent Television

Authority's first ITV franchise began broadcasting, and advertisements were seen on British television screens for the first time. With the formation of a TV news division at the BBC newsreaders Richard Baker, Kenneth Kendall and Robert Dougall presented the first live news broadcasts.

In typically British fashion their early news reports were dominated by the weather as a summer heatwave and associated drought baked the country.

The news turned more serious when Harold Philby held a press conference in London to deny being the 'third man' who tipped off Donald Maclean and Guy Burgess, two of the Cambridge spy ring who had defected to Russia in 1951.

The average house price was a mere £1,900 and unemployment was only 1% of the workforce. Inflation averaged 4%. A new car would cost you around £700, and a gallon of petrol cost 4s 6d (22.5p). Providing you were not *'under the influence of drink or a drug to such an extent as to be incapable of having proper control of the vehicle'* you could enjoy a pint of beer before driving off, which would set you back 9½ old pence. In fact, you could have two or three pints if you wanted, there was no legal drink driving limit until 1967.

Average annual pay was around £434, you would spend about 82 pence a week on groceries, and if you were one of the 14% of households that had a telephone it would cost you £5 to have it installed and a quarterly rental of £3.

In the USA, a salesman named Ray Kroc had seen the potential in a restaurant he supplied and opened the first franchised McDonald's restaurants.

Meanwhile the UK was determined not to be left behind in the transatlantic culinary race as Clarence Birdseye brought fish fingers to the supermarket shelves.

Back across the Atlantic, Rosa Parks was arrested for refusing to give up her bus seat to a white passenger in Montgomery, Alabama, and the civil rights movement in the USA moved up a gear.

In the UK, the BBC broadcast a play titled *'Cap Wil Tomo'* in January 1955. It was the first televised play in the Welsh language, but Wales would have to wait until December 1955 to have an official capital city when Cardiff beat Caernarfon to the title.

The British Army still had a presence in North Africa, especially in Egypt where one young conscript was coming to the end of his National Service. Norman Edgar was a driver and firefighter in the Royal Army Service Corps where he was mostly on standby as the vehicles left by the retreating German Africa Corps in World War 2 were being broken up for scrap. By his own admission Norman spent most of his time… *'sunbathing on top of a fire engine, occasionally extinguishing someone who'd set themselves on fire with a cutting torch'.*

Ten days after celebrating the arrival of 1955 with friends at a formal dance in Bruce Grove, North London, a 25-year-old Administrator working for the Education Committee of the County Council of Middlesex attended an x-ray appointment as part of a workplace mass screening programme for Tuberculosis. Little did she know then how much her life was about to change.

Figure 10 Penny, 1957.

Figure 11

Chapter 10
January 1955

If you walk along the West Green Road, heading away from the A10 Old North Road that has ferried people in and out of London since Roman times, you will find shop fronts that are looking tired, and here and there a boarded over plate glass window where a trade hasn't survived. Not all the young men returned from the last war to carry on family businesses that had passed through generations.

Some shop awnings need replacing and are frayed around the edges, while other more prosperous shops sport gaily coloured canopies that are carefully wound in every night by their exhausted owners.

The bicycle shop is thriving though, and the butchers, with its sawdust floor and little booth for the till, is well stocked now that the austerity of rationing is over.

The rich woody smell from the tobacconists mingles with heady scents from the colourful greengrocers whose produce spills out onto the pavement in neatly packed crates.

A horse drawn cart is still a familiar site on these streets. The rag and bone man is out collecting items to bring back to his mysterious hideaway on the corner of Seven Sisters Road.

A man riding a bicycle pulls a knife grinder behind him, stopping off at the butchers to sharpen knives, then he turns and heads to the green tiled walls and sawdust floor of The Fountain public house to 'wet his whistle'.

You may pass 'Jack' the pigman coming out of Summerhill Road where his piggery is, conveniently close to the slaughterhouse in Philip Lane, or the man who sells horse meat heading towards his pitch on the Wood Green Road.

Trolley buses trundle by, powered by overhead cables that fizz and pop as they go past.

Smoke from a thousand coal fires and factory chimneys lays heavy in the air. On still days the air seems to thicken, and you have to scrape the filth off after a walk to the shops or maybe from watching Tottenham Hotspur play football at White Hart Lane.

Keep walking past houses with bicycles propped against tin dustbins and white Oceana laundry bags left on the red tiles of porchways, waiting for collection; past low walls with the tell-tale rusty stains where iron railings were crudely sawn off to be used for the war effort. Step across Summerhill Road and before you reach Greens Hardware Store with its advertisements for Esso Blue and Aladdin Pink paraffin, turn right at the austere Baptist Church into Dorset Road.

The road is made of worn cobblestones and has a faint air of neglect as little traffic, municipal or otherwise, has cause to use it. The air is dry and dusty and filled with noise thanks to the masonry works that cut the road off abruptly and pen the residents into their own little corner of North London.

On the eastern side are Victorian semi-detached dwellings made of yellow London brick. Numbers 12 and 14 are separated from the road by a low wall and narrow front yard.

Beyond the concrete doorstep of number 14 the door opens into a dingy hall, with a door to the left into a front room dominated by a tailor's dummy swathed in a green satin dress that is being pinned together. The dining table has been taken over by a long ruler, shears and scissors, bolts of cloth and tracing paper, and other paraphernalia of the dress maker's art.

A dusty upright piano has a model head on top wearing a black hat with notes pinned to the side.

Back out in the hallway, steep stairs to the first floor divide the house in two; at the end of the passageway is a further door into the living room.

The first thing that hits you is the smell; smoke, cooking, wet dog, and paraffin. It's not unpleasant exactly, and to the occupants it's an aroma that means comfort, security and home.

This is the hub of the house. Against one wall an old dresser displays plates and crockery that have been handed down or given as wedding gifts.

All horizontal surfaces have been colonised; letters from the hospital and Civil Defence corps, WRVS leaflets, flyers, dance cards, thimbles, and reels of thread.

A large, illuminated radio sits atop a low sideboard. It is powered by a cable plugged into the light socket above.

A gateleg table with three chairs sits next to a bookshelf with a low armchair squeezed into the corner.

The fireplace dominates the far wall, topped by a mantlepiece crowded with photos and postcards propped up against each other, some curling from the heat of the fire and others with corners tucked into the photo frames to keep them in place.

The fire does not 'draw' well and is often lit with the help of a sheet of newspaper stretched over it, which occasionally ignites, to everyone's amusement or consternation, depending on who is holding the flaming paper.

The other wall has a window that looks out to the back garden, and an armchair facing the fire.

A door leads through to a tiny galley style kitchen with painted wooden kitchen units laden with tins, jars, and utensils.

A vivid orange and white curtain suspended under the sink hides cleaning products and an old army ammo box overflows with shoe polish, brushes and rags stained red, brown, and black.

From the kitchen a door opens into the compact back garden with narrow beds of vegetables and a coal store. Beyond the kitchen is the WC and bathroom. It's always cold, even in the heavy, sticky heat of a London summer. The bathroom is only heated on bath nights when the pink paraffin heater is lit, and its fumes fill the house.

Back in the hall and up the stairs the crowded master bedroom is through the door to the left.

A dark heavy wardrobe with a mirror in the middle of three panels reflects the light from the window in the wall opposite. The back wall has a bed with a large, dark headboard, and above it a stern woman stares out of an oval frame hung by wires from the picture rail.

A window behind yellowing nets looks over the street below, and the fourth wall has a dressing table squeezed into the recess next to the chimney breast.

Across the narrow hall at the top of the stairs we walk into the second bedroom. Opposite the door is a window that looks over the garden and into the back gardens of Summerhill Road.

Through another door is the last bedroom. Built above the kitchen and bathroom, its only means of entry and exit is through the second bedroom.

This room has a narrow bed, a bookcase and piles of magazines, a box of tools and car parts, greasy overalls hang from the back of the door and the little wardrobe holds shirts, folded trousers and a couple of suits and ties that hang from the rail.

There is a radio next to the bed with a wire aerial connected to the curtain rail by a crocodile clip; a pair of bakerite earphones have been thrown onto the unmade bed.

Back in the second bedroom the wardrobe doors bulge and are held closed with string tied to the handles. Inside among the office wear and coats are an array of evening dresses and ball gowns.

Boxes of shoes are stacked on the wardrobe floor and balanced on top are hat boxes.

A bookcase is stuffed with sheet music and dance magazines. Most have pieces of paper sticking out. A wind-up record player with dance records in cardboard sleeves stacked against it lays on the floor next to the bed.

Between the window and door to the third bedroom is an untidy desk with a dining room chair pushed in tight and a red exercise book on it. It cost 6d[4].

A woman of 25 years, pale, thin with jet black hair picks up the exercise book and settles herself at her tiny desk. She is gently out of breath after climbing the stairs but would be the last person to acknowledge it.

The room is cold, rain rattles against the thin windowpane and her breath hangs in the air. Downstairs is warm, the fire alight, and the pink paraffin heater warms the front room where someone is humming to herself while sewing a dress.

Up here is private, her brother is away and for a while at least she will be undisturbed. She carefully takes a pen from the pot on the desk and starts to write…

Figure 11 Luigi, Mabel and Penny, back garden of Dorset Road, 1958

---

[4] That's 2½ pence.

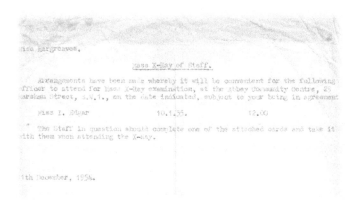

Figure 12

Chapter 11
1955 diary – Selected extracts

January
Rather cold and dull with below average rainfall.

Monday 10
Had mass X-ray this afternoon.

Wednesday 19
I had a note today asking me to attend for a second x-ray at Tooting Grove Hospital…I hope nothing is wrong. Still, what will be will be!

Tuesday 26
I went, this afternoon, to Tooting Hospital (Grove Hosp) to have the second x-ray. I was asked lots of Questions, then x-rayed.

February
Cold, rather dry, and sunny

Wednesday 2
I had a letter this morning from the mass x-ray people at Tooting. Apparently the plate shows some cause for alarm. Dr Browne has been sent the plate and I shall go to him before going to work.
Dr. Browne referred me to Tott. (Tottenham) Chest Clinic – apparently

there is a spot on the left lung. He assures me the T.B. is in its very early stages.

Thursday 3

I'm getting as much as I can cleaned up to-day in case the results of my x-ray are positive.

Friday 4

My appointment at the chest clinic is for 10 o'clock this morning.

I was x-rayed on arrival at the clinic, then made to wait in the dressing cubicle. It was not until 11.30 that I was called to see the doctor. (A very nice young man). He took a blood test and gave me 3 little pots for sputum tests, which have to be handed in at the clinic about next Wednesday. He told me to go to bed (save for meals and toilet) for a fortnight then go to him again when he will be able to tell me whether it is an active spot. He is a very helpful person and did not mind any of my questions re-T.B. He fully explained the x-ray plates to me and I came away much clearer in my own mind about the disease. He gave me permission to go to work this afternoon and get things cleaned up – Mrs. Evans and I cleared everything outstanding – and I came home – about 5 o'clock by 29 bus.

Saturday 5

Doctor Browne read me the report from the chest clinic this morning. There is, as I have already been told, a spot on the left lung which is most probably active. The reason given in the report is the upheaval we've had at home with father.

Sunday 6

My first full day as a T.B. patient! I've read and read and written a couple of letters. Time is not going quite as slowly as I thought it would – thank goodness.

Monday 14

[No diary entry but a letter dated 14.2.55 from a colleague at work. It thanks her for her *'notes and the necessary medicals'*, before updating her on office comings and goings and then descending into some rather cheerful gossip that I dare say wouldn't be sent out by an HR department these days.]

'Sylvia's cold is better although she still has a nasty cough. She has seen her Doc. And he has given her something warming for it.

Ma Evans is still standing around and nattering away. The old bag!

Keep cheery, Iris old dear and let us know what the bosom clinic has to say. I expect you are stuffing food and lapping up quarts of milk – and piling on weight! Ha Ha."

March
Very cold, sunny and dry.

Tuesday 8
Lisa. H. came in…Mum told her I should like to hear all about Germany – like Hell I would!! Mrs. H. was very pleased though. Perhaps she thinks there is still a chance. Though surely nobody would want a T.B. daughter-in-law by choice.

Friday 18
My visit to the clinic this afternoon was quite pleasant. Luckily I was ready very early as the ambulance, having another case at Edmonton at 2 o'clock, called for me at ¼ to 2 instead of ½ past. The Toneograph is nothing much really. One has to stay laying on one's back for about ½ an hour. The Radiographer is very pleasant and he was explaining things to me as he went along. The plate is placed under the table and a little frame with a plate of glass inset and a little orange light behind the glass slides along while one holds one's breath. I suppose this is all an experience!

Saturday 19
The doctor (Browne) had the report on Weds. visit to the clinic. It states that while the lung is progressing my blood still shows activity. A report on the Toneogragh will be sent in due course. Dr. stayed for some time again – this time talking about Religion – He's a most interesting person to talk to.

Sunday 20
I spent this afternoon drawing. What a waste of life this T.B. is! I'm longing to get back to normal, but even then I expect I'll take things steady – this will always be at the back of my mind.

April
Very dry, rather mild and fairly sunny

Saturday 2
Dr. was early today. He still has no report of my Toneogram from the clinic.

Monday 18
Doc. Browne came in this morning. He said he hadn't had a report from

the clinic, so waited until this morning when he rang them up. Anyway, the news was well worth waiting for – the patch is fading!!! I certainly feel much better. Doc. and I usually get on to the subject of theology when he's here – whenever I talk on this subject to everyone else, I always know more than the other person – such is the limited knowledge of my friends about God. Now, here is someone who knows I cannot say to what large extent, much more than me. And how I enjoy our chats. He has helped me a great deal.

Thursday 21

Oh! how I wish I could get out! I feel like a caged animal. Still, this brief confinement has given me more sympathy with prisoners, and I shall definitely take up rehabilitation work when I'm better, if that is at all possible for me.

May
Cool and wet with above average sunshine

Thursday 5

Its surprising how quickly the time is going although I'm in bed all the time. A good thing too!

Wednesday 11

Clinic today! I saw Dr. Mc. Q. himself – a very charming little man. Apparently my "spot" is fading still, and I can now get up for 1 hr. a day for a fortnight, and 2 hrs. a day for the next 2 weeks.

June
Rather cool, dull and wet

Wednesday 8

I saw a new doctor to-day at the clinic (a real dashing type – tall, very dark, and rather handsome). He told me I can now get up for 3 hours a day.

July
Very dry, rather warm and sunny

Saturday 9

Dr. B. had the report from the clinic today. He is disappointed as while the 'spot' is continuing to do well, my blood sed. rate[5] is still too high. It is now 27. So once again I have to take things easily. (sic) It state I shall need 'careful watching!

Sunday 17
This evening – after dark this time – Norman took me for a tiny walk with the dog. Just round Mansfield and back. Even at that time, after dark, we had to dodge people. It isn't really worth while putting one's head out of doors.

August
Very dry and warm with above average sunshine

Wednesday 3
At the clinic this morning I saw the Dr. who is fairly new to the clinic – I don't yet know his name. He is very charming though! However I'm to carry on the same as last month, and can still go out for short walks.

Monday 15
The sister from the clinic called this afternoon, and now I cannot go out at all – just sit in the garden for my 5 hrs.

Tuesday 30
I'm going to the clinic tomorrow, and how I hope everything goes off well!

Wednesday 31
I saw my 'nice' Dr. again this morning at the clinic. (His name is Dr. Pratt-Johnson)[6]. He says I'm over-weight. Also there is a trace of sugar in my waters! Between the two symptoms I've ended up with a most rigid diet. Still, may as well get it all done at once.

September

---

[5] Erythrocyte Sedimentation Rate – a high rate is a sign that inflammation is present in the body.

[6] Dr. John Pratt-Johnson was a bit of a lad. Born in South Africa he went on to specialise in ophthalmology and completed his Post-Graduate Residency in London in 1955. After England and then Scotland he lived in Jamaica before emigrating to Canada. As well as a widely published author of textbooks and setting up his own charitable foundation he was, and I kid you not, Canadian National men's doubles tennis champion in 1992 and Vancouver International Tennis Tournament Champion 2004 (men's singles over 75 years), an avid scuba diver, surfer, accomplished skier, and white-water kayaker. He took up snowboarding and hang gliding when he was 60 years old.

Rather sunny with below average rainfall and near normal temperatures.

Friday 2
Dr. B. called in this morning with the report from the clinic. They've not told him any more than they did me. He asked me to take him a water specimen so he too can make a sugar check!

Sunday 4
Mrs Callier & Eileen came in this evening to ask Mother and I if we would go and sit in her place on Saturday when Eileen gets married. She feels as I do when it comes to trusting folks (not all but some) that live in this road.

Monday 5
I took a specimen of my water to Dr. B. this morning and there was no sugar in it at all – I shouldn't think so after the diet I'm on.

Saturday 10
Mother and I went over to Calliers while they were all at the wedding. We had sat there from 12.30 till about 3 o'clock when we saw Bee and Hal knock at our door. They had come to take me out in their car! Mum went to them and Bee came over to the Calliers. Of course I agreed to go, and what a lovely change it made! We drove out to Hatfield and surroundings. We also took Penny – who insisted on sitting on my lap all the time.

Wednesday 28
Clinic again today! The ambulance was here by ¼ past nine and I wasn't ready!! However, mum took me along by 171 bus.

I saw Dr. Hurst again to-day. He says I'm making satisfactory progress. Still, we shall see what rept. he sends to Dr. B. I've lost 6lbs in weight.

October
Rather cold and sunny with above average rainfall

Sunday 16
When checking the pools this morning we have 21 points on the 7 match treble chance pool. Norman is sending a telegram to claim for us.

Friday 21
Our winnings came from Vernons - £255.13s between Mother and I. This is certainly a Godsend. We are putting together out of this money to buy Norman an overcoat.

Wednesday 26
Clinic day again! I saw Dr. Pratt-Johnson this time. I've lost another 5lbs this last month – I'm beginning to look much slimmer now. Dr. J. told me this morning that although my 'spot' is going on O.K. I might have to go into hospital if they think there is any likelihood of it starting – up again. They may, in that case, give me drugs. Still, as I told him, it isn't really my worry, I'm completely in his hands. I think the whole trouble is the B.S.R.[7]. which is still too high. However I can get up for 7 hours now.

November
Very dry, rather mild and dull

Wednesday 22
Clinic again today! When I saw Dr. Johnson this morning I asked him if I'd misconstrued what he'd said last month. However he said he did tell me that about the hospital, but meant it as a preventative more than a cure. I then told him I should much appreciate a change of scene and he told me he had no objection to my going away – he even suggested the Channel Islands!

He has given me until 4th January to go away.

I went over to see Dr. Browne this evening; he wasn't really too keen on my going to the Channel Islands. Still I shall see Viola on Friday so I think I'll ask her about forms for our Nalgo. Con. Home at Bournemouth.[8]

Thursday 24
I rang Mrs. Evans this morning to tell her my news, and she was very pleased. How very strange it was to use a 'phone again! But then almost everything is strange to me now – in fact I feel quite vague when I go out shopping alone – forgetting what I want in the shops, and crossing the road is hell! Still I must make myself get back to normal again.

Monday 28
Viola rang – and apparently Nalgo Knoles close on the 19th Dec. until 2nd January, and they don't seem too keen on T.B. Patients. However, Viola also rang the National Association for the Prevention of T.B., (N.A.P.T.) and while most of their homes close soon one is still open near Alton, Hants. Viola has arranged for forms to be sent straight away.

---

[7] Blood Sedimentation Rate test.

[8] National and Local Government Officers' Association - trade union. They maintained a convalescent home for their members called Knole Lodge, in Bournemouth.

Tuesday 29

I received my Convalescent Home forms this morning, and I don't really think that Nalgo. is all that suitable. The N.A.P.T. form needs the chest Physician's signature, so I'll take it to the clinic today.

The Welfare Officer took the form from me and told me to leave all arrangements to her. (Suits me!)

December
Mild, rather dry and sunny

Friday 2

I had a letter from the clinic Welfare Officer again today. She offers me a place in a home on the Isle of Wight in February. On thinking it over, I feel this will be the best bet. I went over to the clinic and confirmed this.

I'm glad I did too, as apparently Dr. Johnson recommended it wholeheartedly.

Now I shall have to write to people telling them that I am still home.

Figure 12 X-Ray appointment letter, 1954.

The Mitchley Waltz

1956

'He is nothing more than a bore and a liar!'

The Mitchley Waltz

Figure 13

Chapter 12
An Introduction to 1956

After fleeing Britain in 1951, Guy Burgess and Donald Maclean pop up in Moscow to deny being spies.[9]

In Slough, double yellow lines to prohibit parking appeared for the first time in the UK. If you were handed a hefty fine for a parking violation you could always try your luck winning it back with Premium Bonds, which went on sale for the first time in November, although the first draw for the £1,000 prize didn't take place for another seven months.

Manchester City won the FA cup, notable because their goalkeeper Bert Trautmann was injured 15 minutes from time but played on with what was later diagnosed as a broken neck.

In other health related news, the government declined to lead an anti-smoking campaign, arguing that no ill-effects had been proved.

The iconic Lancaster bomber, famous for its use of 'bouncing bombs' in the 'Operation Chastise' Dam Busters raids of World War 2, flew for the last time in an active role for the RAF.

Fresh from a tour of Nigeria the Queen sauntered up to a remote Cumbrian fishing village to open the world's first commercial nuclear power station at Sellafield.

---

[9] Spoiler alert – they were telling fibs.

Meanwhile Egyptian leader Gamal Abdel Nasser announced the nationalisation of the Suez Canal, which rather peeved her Majesty's Government as well as that of President René Coty of France, triggering the Suez Crisis. France and Britain teamed up for the joint 'Operation Musketeer', in collaboration with Israel, and bombed and seized control of key ports to force the reopening of the canal.

Back home blockades in the Middle East caused the introduction of petrol rationing, and around the world reaction to the Anglo-French operation was overwhelmingly negative. The United Nations General Assembly adopted a resolution calling for *'the United Kingdom, France and Israel to withdraw their troops from Arab lands immediately.'* On 23rd December British and French troops took the hint and left.

In popular culture Bill Haley & His Comets released the seminal Rock Around the Clock, Elvis Presley appeared on the Ed Sullivan show and entered the charts for the first time with Heartbreak Hotel. In the UK Lonnie Donegan promoted his first album, Showcase, and released a cover of Leadbelly's Rock Island Line, which reached number 8 in the charts on both sides of the Atlantic.

In Switzerland Lys Assia won the first Eurovision Song Contest for the host nation with the song Refrain. Great Britain did not take part until the following year, when we came 7th.

If you had enjoyed the animated film of George Orwell's Animal Farm in the cinema the year before, in 1956 you could see the live action version of his dystopian novel 1984, directed by Michael Anderson. Or if you fancied something a little grander in scale, Cecil B. DeMille's The Ten Commandments opened, starred Charlton Heston as Moses. At the time it was the most expensive film ever made.

If you happened to live in St Albans in Hertfordshire or Maldon in Essex, you could help yourself to snacks for your cinema trip in one of the first two self-service Tesco stores in the country.

American company IBM released the first computer with a hard drive, the catchy titled IBM 305 RAMAC. It weighed about one ton and measured 16 square feet.

Also in the United States, a federal court in Alabama ruled that bus segregation laws were unconstitutional. Later in the year the U.S. Supreme Court agreed and declared the Alabama bus segregation laws illegal, but if Rosa Park's protest in Alabama had moved civil rights on, progress was not so quick to catch on elsewhere in the States. In the Kentucky town of Sturgis eight black students were refused entry to Sturgis High School by a mob of white protesters.

Closer to home the 3rd Tottenham Company of the Boys Brigade (BB) celebrated their 40th anniversary in 1956. One of the officers was my father. He was a devotee of the BB and taught the drum and bugle band, as well as taking part in gymnastic displays, organising annual camping trips, and writing sketches for their 'Reviews'.

The Boys Brigade was founded in Glasgow on 4th October 1883 by Sir William Alexander Smith. It claims to be the first voluntary uniformed youth movement in the world, and pre-dates the Scouting movement, which was influenced by it.

In 1956 my parents had yet to meet. My father was an accounts clerk with British Petroleum, working in the city and commuting back and forth from Tottenham. My mother meanwhile was at home busy watching her weight and waiting on an important telephone call…

Figure 13 Leconfield in the snow, 1956.

Figure 14

Chapter 13
Full and unabridged diary for 1956

January
Wet with above normal temperatures and sunshine.

Sunday 1

Today has been equally as uneventful as the rest of this year. I spent the morning altering two skirts. Mother took my measurements before I started and I'm now 36 – 26 – 40. I must get those hips down! The diet has worked wonders, and how grateful I am to Dr. Pratt-Johnson for putting me on it. I shall always have to watch my weight, and avoid any undue strain on my lungs – that won't bother me though!

February
Very cold and dry with normal sunshine

Tuesday 7

I had a letter from the Welfare Officer of the clinic to-day asking me to accept a vacancy in a convalescent home on the I.O.W. (Isle of Wight) from next Monday.

This afternoon Mother and I took Penny to Miss Westbrook's to have her cut, and on the way from there called into the clinic to confirm arrangements for next Monday. Apparently I can get help with the fare, but I mentioned that Norman might take me by car, as he was prepared to do before. She also altered my appt. with Dr. Johnson to tomorrow instead of next Wed.

Norman says I've left it too late for a car, so I shall tell Miss Hetherington tomorrow to go ahead with the train fare business.

We went and collected Penny about 4 o'clock – she looks lovely with her trousers.

Sunday 12

I am now all packed and ready to go away – and how I'm looking forward to the complete change!

Monday 13

I was up early this morning, and left home about 10.15a.m. I was very excited, and yet my feelings were mingled, naturally. Especially as I have never been away from home on my own before. Mother and I arrived at Waterloo in very good time, and she came in the train with me for about ¼ hr. Then the train left at 10 to 12.

The journey was very easy, and the day beautiful. I arrived at Ventnor station about 3.15 p.m. Here were two fellows also going to 'Leconfield' met by taxi. The Fosters are a charming couple, and I feel very much at home here.

After Mrs. Foster had shown me my room – a double room, there is another girl coming in on Wednesday – she introduced me to Dorothy. She is a married woman here with her husband. Then when I'd exchanged pleasantries with her I went down with Mrs. Foster to the dining room, where a cup of tea awaited us.

There are five of us patients here altogether, John and Dorothy, Tony, Bernard and me. They all seem very nice I do hope we all get on well together. This evening we all watched T.V in the lounge. Tony – a most peculiar fellow – showed me all his photographs. They are so tiny they made my eyes ache. I unpacked, and was so tired tonight I didn't bother about being tidy with my clothes.

Tuesday 14

Mrs. Foster took me into Ventnor with her this morning. Before we went I wrote to Mother, just to let her know I'd settled in O.K. As we were leaving John came to us and asked us to get him a Valentines Card for Dorothy. Funny that, because he treats her in a very peculiar way – almost as though she were a child. She runs around after him, and is a proper 'yes-woman'.

This afternoon Mrs. F. took me and Dorothy into Shanklin. We had a lovely afternoon, and Dorothy told us about John and confirmed what I and apparently Mrs. Foster thought. She runs about after him something awful – so much so that when she had T.B. she had to ask to go away because she was still waiting on him, and of course made no progress. We both gave her some advice! And she took it too:- when we got back to Leconfield she called me into her room and showed me the Val. Card which John had put under her pillow. I didn't let on that Mrs. F. and I had bought it. Anyway she laughed like anything about it (she seems to realize that John is all outside show with her) and stuck it back. After tea this evening we all sat round the dining room fire, and John came up to Dorothy and asked her if she'd seen what was under her pillow – she said no, and flatly refused to go upstairs for him again. Mrs. F. and I were much amused – she took our advice at the wrong time!!

This evening we all played Monopoly, and as I came off with a fistful of money they're calling me Lady Docker.[10] They are all pulling my leg unmercifully about Bernard. He is single, 29, and seems very nice indeed. He takes no notice of all these leg-pulls – in fact we both get quite a good laugh out of it all.

Tony is most odd – a ferocious liar, and he has X-ray eyes! I'd not like to trust any woman with him for long.

Wednesday 15

They keep asking me who I'm going to propose to on the 29th – this being a leap year. All the men, Mr. Foster included, want to be on my list of prospective husbands! John says he patrols outside my door all night to keep the others away! We are all getting on famously together. I'm only sorry that Bernard and John and Dorothy have only 2 weeks here and not a month. I fear I shall be left with Tony! But there may be some more patients coming in - I hope!

This morning Tony, who says he knows all the I.O.W., took us into Ventnor. We just strolled round and then had coffee in the Wintergarden. When we got back J and D and I were getting ready for lunch, we had a little conference; and they feel the same about Tony as I do. Wonder how Bernard feels about him! This afternoon Tony showed us another walk around Ventnor. He doesn't know so much about this place as he says. He took us this time along the cliff tops (only a little way though), and we ended this afternoon's expedition in a café having a pot of tea. Then we went for the bus back to Leconfield, and the men bought Dorothy and I a

---

[10] Reference to Norah Lady Docker – In 1949 she married for the 3rd time, to Sir Bernard Docker, chairman of Birmingham Small Arms Company (BSA) and Daimler cars. He built a series of extravagant Daimlers to her specification until he was removed from the board of BSA for extravagant expenses claims, which included cars made available for Lady Docker's personal use, a £5,000 gold and mink ensemble and a castle!

bunch of Jonquils each. Mrs. Foster supplied vases, and they really do make our rooms look like 'home'.

Thursday 16

Mr. Foster brings us tea each morning at about 8.15 a.m. Then breakfast is at 9. Tony is taking us down the Devils Chimney today.

That was a glorious walk, all along the landslips, and then coming back we passed Bonchurch Old Church. Bernard suggested we go and see it. We four must slip out without Tony knowing, because he is nothing more than a bore and a liar! After leaving the landslip we went to Bonchurch and just up on the low cliffs there, then into the village for a pot of tea – then we had a taxi back to Leconfield.

This afternoon Tony showed us the way into Shanklin – by bus – and from there we took the cliff path to Sandown. When we were leaving to come back to Ventnor a slight mishap occurred! We saw the times of the buses and realized we should be late back at Leconfield for tea. So while Tony, J and D went to the toilet, B and I said we'd nip up to the station and find out the times of the trains. When we got back to the bus stop they had gone – apparently we thought back by bus. But no! We rang Mrs. Foster to explain why we were late, then up to the station again, only to find the others waiting outside there. Tony had shown them a short cut! That man will have to go!

Friday 17

It was snowing this morning when I woke up – but it still isn't cold. J and D have decided not to go out this morning, however B and I are still going. I wrote a letter home first, then at 10.30. we both slipped out of the room, like a pair of fugitives, and went out as quietly as possible, so that Tony shouldn't know. Bet we'll get plenty of ribbing when we get back. When we got to the Church, we applied for the key only to be told it didn't open until Easter – still we had a lovely walk together through the landslip. We two get on very well together. How surprised we were when we got back and Tony had nothing to say! Perhaps he's cross – I think he'd like to take me out, and resents me going with Bernard. It didn't snow for long and I felt much better for going out. John told me that Tony said he wouldn't be coming out with us again, he hadn't any money. Then he told Bernard that he'd come with us if there was another woman – what are we to believe!

We stayed in this afternoon and Tony taught us to play crib – but we couldn't follow the game as he showed us, but Mr. Foster says he'll show us some time or other.

Saturday 18

It was very bright this morning and Bernard suggested we go up top – following the Wroxall footpath. J and D are not coming, Dorothy isn't too well, I feel – still they are going out this afternoon with us. It was a straight climb up the downs. We kept stopping to rest; and when we got to the top by the Radio Station was it windy! However we eventually reached Wroxall – and for the first time for over a year we ran for a bus! It was a glorious walk, and I feel so 'at home' with Bernard.

B, J and D. are talking about applying to their clinics for another 2 weeks. I do hope they get them.

This afternoon we four went into Shanklin – we walked through Luccombe Common. There is a vast change in the area owing to landslides and coast erosion – the place seems quite altered since I was last here about 5 years ago. It began to snow again on the way to Shanklin, but it was only showers, and on the whole the weather was very bright.

John bought some tobacco in a little shop in Old Shanklin Village, and I bought a book on walks on the Island, for B and I are going to see as much of the place as we can – and if he gets his other fortnight I don't think there will be any holding us! We went into the Black Cat Café, and passed a most pleasant time, then John decided his Tob. was hard, and took it back to the shop to change it, while B and I went to get a film in the chemist. Well, we missed each other again, and decided that the tobacconist must have done some terrible things to J and D., but no! We saw them, looking for us, by the bus stop – heaven alone knows how we missed each other.

There was boxing on T.V. this evening, and J and Tony were in their element – but B. D. and I didn't relish looking at it so we went into the dining room, Dorothy asked us if we minded all the leg-pulling – and we assured her that we take no notice whatever – a fact that pleased her no end.

Sunday 19

It was a lovely bright sunny day again to-day, with no sign of snow, and B and I decided on doing one of the walks in the book I'd bought. We started from Ventnor Station and went up zig-zag road until we picked up the Whitwell Road – then on to the cliff path, to St. Lawrence. A little later St. Catherine's Lighthouse came into view. Our way led all through fields of sheep, cattle, and farms in general. It was really wonderful, and I felt a terrific sense of satisfaction. It was very windy, and so high that at times I felt giddy. We eventually reached Niton, a pretty little inland village. Another mishap - we forgot that the buses are all 'up the spout' on Sundays. We couldn't find Fosters in the telephone directory, so just had to catch the 1 o'clock bus back to Ventnor and hope for the best. Anyway we decided that we shall do a picnic if the weather holds, then we can go as far as we like without having to rush back. We went into Randall's for a taxi back to Leconfield as it was late, but there was no sign of anyone there, so after waiting for almost five minutes we walked back, arriving indoors about ¼ to 2. We had our dinner on our own, and Fosters were very good about us being late back. Of course we had our legs pulled dreadfully.

Monday 20

Bernard has written to his Almoner[11] asking for extra time – we have told John to do the same, or he will leave it too late. It snowed heavily during the night and this morning it is laying quite thick on the roads. Leeson Hill is very dangerous.

We went into Ventnor this morning via Bonchurch – it was most picturesque there covered in snow. We took some snaps, which if they come out should be beautiful.

When we got to Ventnor Bernard, following Johns suggestion, went to see the British Legion people to see if they can help him with the extra 2 weeks, should his Almoner be unable to do anything.

We four went into Ventnor again this afternoon, and got talking about this time last week, when we all first met and were weighing each other up. Bernard said he thought I was posh, and wouldn't talk to me in case I'd not answer him! J and D asked us to go to stay with them at Redhill.

We all played cards this evening. It is still snowing heavily.

Tuesday 21

Bernard rang his Almoner this morning, and as she wasn't there her assistant told him the Almoner would ring back after 11 o'clock. So we had to stay in this morning. It gave me a chance to write some letters and cards though. I had 2 lots of parcels this morning – first Olive sent me some writing materials and some "Ideal Home" books, then my other clothes came from Mother. When Bernard's Almoner rang back she said the council wouldn't grant him the extra time but that she was trying another channel.

This afternoon B and I walked into Shanklin, all along the bus route – the snow was very deep, in fact it was in drifts along part of the road. We went into the Black Cat for afternoon tea, and then down on the beach to take snaps in the snow. We caught the bus back to Leconfield.

John and Tony tried to teach us to play Solo this evening, but it seems mighty complicated to me.

---

[11] Almoner – distributor of Alms – I think Bernard's therapeutic holiday was sponsored by his local authority, as was my mothers. The Almoner in this instance would be a broker akin to a modern-day Social Worker.

Wednesday 22

The snow is still deep, although it is much warmer. B and I planned to meet Dorothy and John in Ventnor Post Office. While we were waiting for them I took quite a good snap by the cinema of the roof tops in the snow. Bernard changed Tony's insurance money for him so that he wouldn't accompany us onto Ventnor. We went in and had our usual coffee. I sincerely hope these people get their extra time.

This afternoon B and I rode into Shanklin and walked from there all along the cliff path into Sandown. It was glorious and exhilarating, but so windy! When we got into a café in Sandown my face muscles were frozen; or so they seemed. The thaw seems to really be on the way now.

Thursday 23

Bernard went down into Ventnor this morning to see the British Legion folks – I was going to meet him down there, but Leeson Hill was so very icy I decided not to take the hill on my own. I didn't go down with him because if they saw him with a woman they might not help him at all; thinking that I and not health was his reason for wanting extra time here. Anyway while he was out news came through that he has been granted another week by his council – that means he will stay the extra 2 weeks – he was prepared to pay for one week by himself. I cannot express my pleasure – I'm so very grateful for this extension. I'm keeping my fingers crossed now for John and Dorothy.

This afternoon we decided to try and find the look-out post, and sure enough we passed it before. There is a lovely view from there, all over tree tops to the sea. It is beginning to turn much warmer.

Friday 24

John, Dorothy, Bernard and I went into Newport this afternoon. It was a dreary place, and seemed much colder than Ventnor, by many degrees. There is another married couple coming in on Monday – wonder what they will be like? While in Newport I had a look round for Norman's camera, but couldn't see one that appealed.

Saturday 25

We took the bus to Ryde this afternoon, and I again had a look round for Norman's camera. This morning I saw one in Shanklin – a Kershaw – which I think is just the job. There wasn't much time in Ryde, and we soon had to catch our bus home – we really must allow ourselves more time!

Sunday 26

Bernard and I took the cliff walk from Ventnor, past Flowers Brook and along to St. Catherine's Point. We didn't leave ourselves enough time to get back by 5.30 and had a dreadful rush. When we did get back we found that tea was 6 o'clock tonight instead of 5.30. There was no need to have rushed at all.

This morning we explored Bonchurch – especially round the beach – its really delightful.

The weather is very lovely.

Monday 27

We decided to go to Blackgang Chine this afternoon, but after lunch we found we had left it too late for the bus from Ventnor – however we did try and catch it, but to no avail. So we took John and Dorothy part of the walk we did yesterday afternoon.

When we got back to Leconfield we found Tony in his element with the new couple - Ron and Kit. B and I cannot stand them, and I felt really out of it all evening, so apparently did Bernard. We all played Housey Housey. I'm wondering what J and D think of them – I've an idea they don't mind them.

Tuesday 28

Bernard and I cannot make out whether J and D prefer to be with Kit and Ron or us. Tony took Kit and Ron out this morning after we'd gone out – and it appears J and D went with them to the Lookout Post. B and I went to Boots and ordered Norman's camera – I finally decided on the Kershaw. Then we had coffee and walked back to Bonchurch along the cliffs.

We ordered a taxi to take us down to the buses this afternoon (making sure we didn't again miss our bus for Blackgang) and then went all over the Chine. We were the only two people there, and the scenery can only be described as majestic! We left the Chine after a while and went to a landslip nearby. Climbing about there was like Commando training, but it was wonderful.

There was quite a thick mist at Blackgang – but it was a pleasant sea mist.

Wednesday 29

Bernard went to the Barbers this morning and I bought my wrapping paper and cotton wool to pack the camera in. It hasn't arrived yet, but may do by the later post. While B. was in the barbers I went back to Leconfield with my wares, and collected a parcel of B's. and went to meet him in Bonchurch. While I was back at Leconfield Mr. Foster asked me if there was anything between B and I. I assured him there wasn't, and he seemed quite relieved – funny that!

I met B. in Bonchurch. He had met J and D who told him they too were not keen on Ron and Kit, but felt they must mix with them. They had given them the slip this morning so we two returned to Ventnor and found J and D in our usual café and we all four had a good discussion – and arranged tomorrow as our day for the trip round the island. The others rode back, but B and I went into Randall's and booked the car for tomorrow, then walked back to Leconfield.

This afternoon B and I went into Shanklin, and walked through America Woods – it was gorgeous. We came back into Shanklin and had our tea in a nice little café – complete with soft music!

J. and D. went to the pictures this evening with K. and R. We played cards with Tony!

Figure 14 Sandown beach in the snow 1956.

Figure 15

March
Dry, sunny and rather mild.

Thursday 1
Our day round the island was most successful. We had our lunch in the Needles Hotel, Alum Bay. The sandwiches went down very well with a glass of Cider. The weather was again kind to us and how tired I was by the time we got back to Leconfield.

Friday 2
Norman's camera is at last in at Boots! B. and I went into Ventnor this morning to collect it, and then studied it well over our morning tea. I'm very pleased with it – and think Norman will be too – I hope!

This afternoon we went into Shanklin to do a spot of shopping, and this evening learned to play Gin Rummey. (sic) It promises to be a most interesting game.

Saturday 3
We took the footpath from Shanklin to Ventnor this afternoon, and was it windy! We had to hold on to each other to get along at all – it would have been very easy to get blown over. We came out by Ventnor Station – the climb down Boniface Down there is very very steep, but after a lot of sliding about we made it into Ventnor.

We explored Bonchurch Beach further this morning and found it has possibilities of a walk into Shanklin from there when the tide is low.

However we came up at Rylstone Village – by Luccombe, and walked back to Leconfield.

Sunday 4

This morning B. and I. went up Nansen's Hill, after first visiting the lookout post again. It was a lovely clear morning and we could see right across the island to the mainland - i.e., Portsmouth, Southampton, and even beyond that. We stood there for sometime by the Ordinance Survey Triangulation Station not wanting to leave, but had to eventually. On the way down we got lost and ended up on a hill covered in trees, merging into a slope of solid mud! We always find mud. We came out by Cowleaze Hill, and were only about 15 mins. late for dinner.

This afternoon we went along Bonchurch beach into Ventnor, ending up in the Briantree[12] for tea before going back to Leconfield.

Monday 5

B. and I. did our first picnic today. We got to Freshwater, from there walked to Alum Bay, where we had our lunch, and then on to Tennyson Downs – back through Torland to Freshwater. We missed the bus back to Newport we had planned to catch, but just didn't care. We had a pot of tea in a dear little café in Freshwater – eventually arriving back at Leconfield about 6.15. It was nice having our meal together after such a lovely day.

Tuesday 6

It is cold and windy today – B. and I. went to the post office to get Norman's camera off, while J. and D. went into the cloisters. They met us by the café for coffee.

This afternoon we (B and I) went up to the Triangulation Station again. Bernard asked me to marry him when we are both completely cured – but I pointed out that although we are a perfect match I have no guarantee of a permanent cure, while he has, having had an op. He agreed of course – so no human element is allowed at the moment. I cannot imagine marriage with anyone though.

Wednesday 7

B. and I. are off on another picnic today. This time we went into Ryde, then had coffee in the Galleon – what a lovely café it is! Pink lights, etc. from there we walked to Seaview; and what a disappointment that place was. After having lunch we explored – and how dilapidated it is there now! It has gone downhill fast since 1951 when I was last there. Then we went through Nettlestone back to Ryde. Then back into the Galleon for tea. We

---

[12] Briantree Hotel, Albert Street, Ventnor.

met J. and D. at Ryde station - they'd been to Portsmouth – and we all returned to Leconfield together. They were most disappointed with Portsmouth, but we had a good laugh over it.

This evening Ron, Bern, John and I played Gin Rummy in the dining room.

Thursday 8

We took snaps this morning on the lawn at Leconfield of the folks we've been staying with – then we took them into Ventnor.

In the café over coffee Bernard said he never regretted anything so much as this holiday ending – he isn't the only one! I shall miss him tremendously.

This afternoon we both walked over Wroxhall Downs, and it was lovely laying in the long grass. The sun was warm and I could have stayed there forever.

Then this evening we spent the time with J. and D. in Bonchurch Inn. A real little country Inn, and I've not enjoyed an evening out so much.

Friday 9

Into Ryde this morning, and of course The Galleon. Then we walked into Fishbourne, via Quarr Abbey. We should both like to live in Fishbourne. Then on to Wooton and back to Ryde and The Galleon.

A perfect day!

My own friends seem very smug, stuffy to me now. Bernard keeps teasing me about having to go to chintzy tea parties! We walk about criticising the houses and discussing the bungalow we shall have – I wonder though, will we ever be able to!

I've had an awful pain in my back today.

Saturday 10

We caught the bus from Shanklin to Bembridge this morning and walked from there to Whitecliff Bay. Then we climbed up Culver Cliff and lay there in the sun for about an hour. I had another nasty pain again today – hope nothing is wrong.

Sunday 11

Into Sandown today, and walked inland to Alvestone and Yarbridge. We topped off our holiday in the Bonchurch Inn this evening.

I cannot say when I've enjoyed anything so much as this holiday. Or when I've been so sorry to see the back of a male companion. But Bernard was so different – he never made any advances to me, even when we were entirely alone in the wilds. And he thought quite something of me, I know. I did appreciate that. Then we had no other person to please, because what suited one suited the other – we agreed so very very well. Holidays are going to seem so very dull again – especially if I'm with someone who doesn't want to climb, or who wants to look in shops, or sit in deckchairs.

Monday 12

Home today! We caught the 9.40 train from Ventnor. I know I'm going to miss Bernard, but we shall be in touch. Mother met me at Waterloo – it was nice to see her again. Penny and Luigi are much the same as ever, only that Luigi has moulted and looks ever so scabby.

I suppose I must now think about getting back to work – Dr. Guri has asked the Principle of Tottenham Technical College to consider me for a post in the office there. I shall like that very much.

Tuesday 13

I've developed an awful pain in my left side – but I'm going to Dr. B. this evening about my certificate so will ask him about it.

This afternoon Mother came with me to Wood Green and I bought a pair of red pumps, and handbag and gloves to match.

Dr.B. advised me to bring my clinic appointment forward.

Wednesday 14

I went to the clinic this morning, and Dr. Johnson saw me without prior appt. My weight has dropped from 11st. 9 lbs. to 10st. 12 lbs.[13] during the past month. Dr. J. was very worried about my x-ray. He said there must still be a bug left from the old spot which has spread thus:-

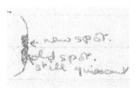

Figure 16 – Diary extract.

So now I've got to go into hospital as soon as can be arranged.

In the meantime I'm to go to bed again and the district nurse is to give me drugs at home.

Still, I have that wonderful month to look back on: and I'm not really sorry this has happened because it will mean a guaranteed cure. As Dr. J. pointed out I'd have broken down soon after I got back to work, so I'm glad it happened now.

---

[13] 73.9 kg down to 64.2 kg

Thursday 15

I had a letter from Bernard this morning – it was just like reading one of my own letters – funny how we are so much alike! He said to meet him and his Mother next Thursday to go to the Ideal Home Exhibition. Anyway I wrote and gave him my news - wonder how he'll take it.

The electricians have been today seeing to the faulty lights.

Friday 16

The sister from the clinic came in today for a little chat. I feel much better about going into hospital now I've seen her. In fact I'm going to have a good time – I've made my mind up on that score.

Saturday 17

Another letter from Bernard this morning – he was most reassuring about hospital. He also mentioned marriage again – seems he doesn't mind a wife who is likely to be an invalid.

Norman collected my last photos from Gainsboroughs. They have again turned out quite good -I must put them all in my album.

Saturday 24

Norman's 21st birthday- goodness how the years have flown by! He was thrilled to bits with the camera; I thought he would be. Instead of holding a party he is going to have a few friends in tomorrow morning for a drink.

Sunday 25

Dick called in this morning, but didn't stay long as I'm not supposed to be tired – in fact I am not really allowed visitors yet.

Then Norman's pals arrived, and two girls who came up to see me. Bright specimens to be sure! But not so bad as I had expected. What if Norman eventually goes seriously with that type of girl. Still, they'll settle down perhaps.

Friday 30

Aunty Dol came this evening! She seemed ever so pleased to see me again, and I was glad to see her once more. She's so funny, and I'm sure she doesn't realize it. She was hilarious about Aunty Alice who is marrying Harry Long on 23rd April. She wants to come into the hospital to see me, but I'm afraid I shall laugh so much when she's there, that either she or I will get turned out.

Figure 15 John, Dorothy, Tony & Bernard, Ventnor, 1956.

Figure 17

April
Cold and dry with below average sunshine

Wednesday 4

Em. came today. She was more pleasant than I expected her to be. I showed her my snaps – but still don't think she really grasped them. Still, I like looking at them again myself – so not to worry!

I really must get down to some letter writing, but honestly don't feel like doing anything. I feel really queer this time, and even washing is a terrific exertion.

Saturday 7

A letter from Bernard this morning returning my snaps.

Mrs. Calver called over for a few minutes this afternoon – it made a nice change to see her again. I don't really want to see people though.

Sunday 8

A surprise this afternoon! Edna came, as she hadn't heard from me and she wondered what was happening to me. We spent quite a pleasant afternoon together. But as she was going she said how people at the dances still ask after me, and how when they heard I was away convalescing they said "good – she will be back dancing again".

I then told Edna that I'd not dance again – but she couldn't grasp the fact that it wouldn't appeal to me again, and tried to 'cheer' me up by saying - "Don't be silly, lots of people have had T.B. that go dancing". I let it pass!

It will sink in eventually when I'm about again and still do not go.

This type of illness alters one's whole conception of life!

Monday 9

I walked down the garden this morning – and oh! how well everything is doing! The Wisteria is in bloom and also the muscari and hyacinths.

Mrs. H. put her head over the gate, and cried when she saw me. Auto-suggestion because I still look o.k.

Tuesday 10

Violet Wight came up to see me this afternoon, and we spent a very good time together. She's very bright, and it made a lovely change. Then this evening Jean came. Either all or none! It was good to see her again; and I believe my prayers for her are now being answered. She is still 'carrying-on' with L. Donnigan (sic) but she tells me he is going to America for 10 weeks. Well a lot can happen in that time!

Wednesday 18

This morning my awaited letter arrived! I go into St. Ann's tomorrow the 19th – at last! I spent the day packing and getting myself ready in general. Now I'm quite looking forward to hospital.

Thursday 19

The ambulance came for me this morning at 10.a.m. It was hard to leave Penny and Luigi again, but this time I am hoping to have a permanent cure. On arrival at the hospital I was put into a bed in a large ward of 20 patients – it is split into small bays of 4 patients. I am in with 3 very nice girls. Dr. Johnson came around this afternoon together with a dark Indian Doctor, and they told me I start treatment on Monday. I'm going to go on Streptomycin and Iona[14]. These girls that I'm with make me feel at home already, and the nurses are extremely kind.

Mother came along this evening to see me settled.

Friday 20

I slept very well last night, although it was my first night away. This hospital isn't all it's cracked up to be! The floors are dirty – windows are dirty, even the cutlery and some crockery!

I shall get my own cutlery brought in.

Vera, one of the girls in my bay is going for a big x-ray today. I have been given some sputum pots, but cannot produce anything. Perhaps they'll take some from me. We've a funny (in a peculiar and humorous way)

---

[14] Isoniazid

cleaner. Her name is Liz, and she's the most amusing creature I have come across in a long time.

Norman came in this evening with Mother.

Saturday 21

I am still sleeping well, and am now very settled. There is an Irish girl, Mary, in my bay and she's a R.C. She found I was interested in Roman Catholicism and asked the Priest to have a word with me. He came over and said he'll bring me in some literature. Aunty May came to see me.

Sunday 22

I still cannot produce any sputum, but the Nurse this morning said they'll take it from me. I shall be examined tomorrow by Dr. Bowes- the Indian Doctor.

We are on complete bed rest – when we want the toilet we are taken in a wheelchair.

Edna came with Mother this afternoon. I'm quite enjoying my stay here; and dressing myself up in smart type pyjamas, which helps the morale very much.

Monday 23

A 'busy' day today! They didn't give me any drugs today. I had an x-ray (we're taken by van to the x-ray unit). Then after dinner we had a bath - screens are put round each bed and we bath on the bed between blankets – then Dr. Bowes examined me. He gives a very through exam, and when he told me that if it wasn't for my lung I'm in perfect health, I felt very bucked. He says I must have a gastric lafarge[15] (sic) tomorrow to take my sputum.

Tuesday 24

The sister came along first thing this morning to take my sputum. I thought it would be an awful experience, but it was only uncomfortable. A rubber tube is passed up the nose and then it falls down the throat, and the sputum is drawn up from the stomach.

Then this morning Nurse Duggan gave me my first Strep. injection, and I also had my first Iona tablets. These drugs make me feel very dopey. Norman came with Mother this evening, and he's got his new teeth – they are lovely – very natural.

Wednesday 25

I had my second gastric lafarge this morning – and my second load of drugs. When Mother came in this afternoon I was ever so dopey. During

---

[15] I think she misheard – presumably, a gastric lavage, commonly known as a stomach pump.

rest hour we had a very good laugh – Mary has new glasses and cannot see out of them, we all tried them on, throwing them from bed to bed.

Friday 27

Iris had her bronchogram[16] this morning.[17] Our injections were rather painful this morning – a different nurse gave us them. My leg feels so heavy now. Norman came in with Mother this evening.

Saturday 28

I feel very well today – so does Vera. We have been wearing St. Philomena's card[18] and it certainly makes a difference. Mary played the Gramophone this afternoon, and we all felt very bright. I'm now a confirmed Philomena follower.

Monday 30

Jean came in this evening – she's a silly girl, still depressed over Lonnie Donnigan.

Figure 17 Iris, St Ann's hospital, 1956.

---

[16] *"Air bronchogram refers to the phenomenon of air-filled bronchi (dark) being made visible by the opacification of surrounding alveoli (grey/white). It is almost always caused by a pathologic airspace/alveolar process, in which something other than air fills the alveoli".* radiopaedia.org.

[17] I don't know if she was referring to herself in the 3rd person or if there was another Iris in her bay. Maybe it was the drugs?

[18] St. Philomena was born around 291 in Corfu and died aged 13 in Rome. Her remains were discovered in 1802. Several miracles have been accredited to her. She is the patron saint of infants, babies, and youth.

ES OR FACTORIES AT

40 YEARS OLD — AND
STILL GOING STRONG

HE LIKES
GERMANY

'You'll get no mercy,'
warns Sessions Chairman

Figure 18

May
Very dry, sunny and rather warm

Tuesday 1

This evening Mrs. Evans came to see me with Mother. As I'd not seen Mrs. E. for some time Mother went and talked to Mary. What I thought was so very kind was Hilda Whanton sent a box of chocolates.

Wednesday 2

Mother came in this morning – I was half asleep when she came in. Surprise upon surprise! She had a letter from Bernard this morning to say he's coming to see me. Mother and he have been in touch for a few days, unbeknown to me! Of course Mother and I haven't had any chance to talk much this last few nights as I've had so many other visitors. And although she comes with them we cannot discuss any private arrangements in front of strangers. Anyway, Mother told B. to get to West Green by 76 - and then when he wrote to her he said Wood Green, so she came in to confirm the matter, but I couldn't help her because I've not heard from him.

Anyway, after Mother "solicited" several men, she eventually found the right one – Goodness knows what she thought of him. It was nice seeing him again; and I did appreciate him coming all that way. He came up by coach. I was terribly dopey with the strep, but I don't think he minded.

Thursday 3

The docs. came round this morning, and Dr. Johnson gave me some wonderful news. My new spot is in an even earlier stage than my other one, and the x-ray I had last week shows an improvement already. I feel very very happy about this. I know Mother will be pleased too.

Viola and Olive came along this evening. This was the first time since about Xmas since I've seen them – and it was very pleasant being with them. Olive looked better than she's looked for sometime, she had a new grey suit on that she's made, and it suits her well. Mother went and sat with Vera; but I didn't mind, as she doesn't have many visitors.

Friday 4

When Mother came in this evening she was here about 10 mins. when Rene came, Rene looks very well now, and was bright and full of beans. Mother seems very relieved about my good report of yesterday.

Saturday 5

I had a letter from Bernard this morning – he says how much he enjoyed his visit and also how much he liked my Mother. However, I don't think Mother was keen on him! She hasn't mentioned him to me at all – I bet she thinks we are serious, and is disappointed in my choice! Anyway she's wrong. There is, of course, nothing between us, and I'm glad there isn't as she isn't keen.

Sunday 6

We have been pulling Mary's leg about Norman today. Poor Mary! I do believe that sometimes she takes me seriously. And when Norman walked in – Mary's face was a picture.

Tuesday 8

Edith came with Mother this evening. She looks so well it's unbelievable. I was so glad she came, among other reasons because it will give Vera a good heart for her operation. Edith is very bright and happy, but she well deserves to be after all she has been through.

Wednesday 9

Mrs. Parker came over this afternoon with Mother at visiting, then Nan came in about 10 mins later. Poor old Nan – she started talking about cancer! She'll never alter! However, she and Mrs. Parker got on very well; in fact, Mrs. P. seemed quite taken with her.

Thursday 10

More good news this morning from the doctors. However, they are going to give me a sugar test, my B.S.R. still being high. Dr. Johnson said that if I go on as I am now he will start getting me up in a months time. Poor Mary was told that she is to have a bronchogram – there is evidently some question of surgery.

Mother didn't come tonight, but Viola and Olive came along. Olive brought me some lovely red roses, they're beautiful.

Friday 11

When Mother arrived this evening Aunty May was waiting outside. So again I couldn't see Mother on her own. But it was good to see Aunty May – she's very funny, especially over Aunt Ad. Mother says she won't be in tomorrow as Em. has booked her up to go down to her – poor Mother!

Meanwhile, a certain Mr. Don Canham was pictured in the local paper on 11 May with the 3rd Tottenham Company of the Boys Brigade…(see figure 18 at the beginning of this chapter).

Saturday 12

Today has passed much the same as usual. This is a peculiar sort of life in hospital! But; I really do believe that God has taken away my life; which I loved, to bring me nearer to him. And this illness has brought me nearer – I think I shall eventually turn Catholic; but it is something on which I think I shall feel quite definite.

Norman came in this evening – he came in on his bike which he's now painted bright green! Its always nice to see him.

Sunday 13

Mother, Edna and Connie came in this afternoon. We all had a good laugh at Nan's doings yesterday. I still haven't had my sugar test yet.

I've sent off for details of several correspondence courses, on various subjects – perhaps when I go home I shall be able to go into some different employment – still with the Middx. Ed. Committee.

Tuesday 15

This morning I wasn't allowed anything to eat until 10.30 – They were giving me a sugar test. Dr. Bois took a blood test at 7.30 and I had to use the bed pan then and drink a glass of glucose! I've never tasted such awful sickly stuff in my life. Then every half-hour I had a blood test and had to use the bed-pan for a urine test. Then at 10.30 all was finished, and I had an egg and a pot of tea and toast!

Thursday 17

Dr. Johnson told me today that there was no sugar at all in my tests. And that if my x-ray is O.K. next week, he will start grading me – provided my B.S.R. is down. I have been giddy now for some days, I think it's the Strep.

Friday 18

Mary goes for her bronchogram this morning. When Mary came back from her x-ray she was fine. In fact, this evening she got up and went down to Josie's bay for sometime. The only thing is she might overdo it.

Saturday 19

Mary was queer today – she seems to be in a fever. The nurse told Dr. Bois about my giddiness, and he came to see me – he has taken me off Strep. And from tomorrow I am to go on Diomycin.[19]

Sunday 20

Mary is very ill today! She has a temperature of 102.

Dick came in this afternoon, just after Mother had arrived. He's a nice old character.

Monday 21

Mary is very, very ill. She keeps vomiting, but hasn't eaten anything. She must feel awful.

I weighed 10st. 11.4oz. to-day. I have lost 14 ounces. I'm not bothered though, I think it must be the drugs affecting me. Dr. Bois came to see me when he went to Mary, and told me to keep on with Diomycin, and see how I go.

Tonight Mary was dreadful, but no one seems to bother, and we are so very helpless. Anyway, Sister Henson rang the Doc. and he says Mary has a touch of pneumonia! Poor Mary!

Tuesday 22

Mary was moved into a cubicle this morning – that is what she needs – she must rest. She isn't allowed any visitors, and has to lay on her right side to let the fluid drain from her left lung.

I am still terribly dizzy, and Nurse Duggan spoke to Dr. Bois about me, and he says I'm not to have any drugs tomorrow at all, and then on Thursday he and Dr. Johnson will decide what's to be done with me.

Figure 18 Cutting from Edmonton Weekly Herald, 11May 1956.

---

[19] A broad-spectrum antibiotic.

Figure 19

July
Very wet, rather cool and dull

Thursday 5

The gap in my diary is caused through my being very ill on the drugs. Dr. Johnson tried me on 4 types of P.A.S[20] after taking me off Strep. and Diomycin. However I couldn't take any of it, and then Sister came back from Scotland and put me back on P.A.S Granules (Bird Seed), and I've been on them for about 4 weeks; and thank God can keep them down.

As soon as Sister came back – the same day in fact-she moved me into a cubicle with Mary Keilthy! This is what we've wanted all along – we are very happy in here. Also I'm studying German, French and Italian, and of course find the quietness of a cubicle grand. I'm also now allowed to work with oil paints – my first effort is for Mary.

Dr. Bois has left the ward, his place being taken by a sweet little lady-Dr. Butterworth – who after a couple of weeks also left – her place being taken by another woman, Dr. Greenburgh. We've not yet seen her, but she will most probably be round today with Dr. J. Father Smith has also left, and we are now visited by a charming newly-ordained Priest of about 23 or 24[21]. I like him even better than Father Smith.

Saturday 21

I've still got no grading, but hope to have one soon. Dr. J. told me Thursday that I'm doing well on the P.A.S., but that he wants me to go back on Strep. in a month or so's time. What a business this all is.

I had a letter from Bernard and he says he's back at work – he sounds so thrilled with himself and expects me to be just as pleased – he still thinks our futures are tied-up together – how wrong he is, but I must find a way to let him know he's wrong without hurting his feelings – poor old devil![22]

---

[20] PASER (PAS) granules - a chemotherapeutic agent used in the treatment of TB.

[21] Father John Harrington – we'll be meeting him again soon.

Thursday 26

Dr. Johnson gave me a bathing grade to-day. I wonder if I shall be grading each fortnight! Also he told me I am to go back on Diomycin twice a week. I hope and pray I shall be able to take it this time.

Monday 30

I had my first Diomycin injection this morning. My weight has gone up now to 11 stone exactly. My language courses are still going strong, and now that Mary is out each afternoon I am able to give from 2 to about 4 to study.

Figure 19 Mabel & Iris.

---

[22] I was looking through her photo albums and the Isle of Wight features heavily. A couple of portraits of her sitting on a bench have obviously been cut down, although she had still taken the time to mount them along with the others. They both clearly say 'Bernard and me, I.O.W 1956' on the back in her handwriting. Quite why she cut him out of the photo but still went to the trouble to mount them beside others that were almost the same but with just her in, I shall never know.

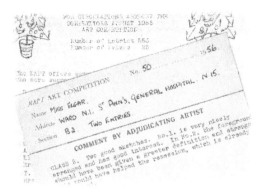

Figure 20

August
Very cool, wet and rather dull

Thursday 2
My second injection to-day. So far so good. Doc. J. was pleased at my being able to take the drug.

Monday 6
My weight is now 10.13.15 – 1 ounce lost! Heaven. I hope sincerely that I don't get too heavy again. Another injection today.

Tuesday 7
Ann washed my hair for me today – she gives it a very good wash always. Mother has got me a beautiful white lacy blouse for Edna's birthday – but I shall have to give it to her when I next see her as she is in Bournemouth at the moment.

Thursday 9
I wondered if I'd get my walk to-day, but Doc. J. said – "no more grades for you yet" – so there we are! He did say that I am now to go on injections every day starting tomorrow.

Tuesday 14
My birthday! And although in hospital it went off really well. We invited all the girls from the cubicles – i.e. Kitty Butcher, Phyliss Kitchenside, Joan Chick, Doris Trover, Sheila Hall. The only one from the ward was Kate Schrubshall. Then we invited all the staff in. My cake was lovely – all pink – and Norman had brought me a goodly supply of drinks.

I had some lovely gifts including:-
- A white woollen stole from Viola.
- Lily of the Valley talc. and Perfume from the Office.
- A lovely peach coloured make-up box and a peach coloured nightie from Mother and Norman.
- A beautiful Sacred Heart Prayer Book from N.1.[23]
- "Red Shoes for Nancy"[24] – from Mary and Joan.
- A pair of earrings like open orchids from Connie.
- Biro and Desk Pad from Edna.
- A pearly white brooch from Nan.
- A Lily of Valley Twistick from Mrs. MacBurnie.
- Stationery from Olive
- Stationery from Miss Williamson.
- Stationery from Sylvia and George.
- Black Rose Talc from Jean.
- 37 Cards.

In the evening Olive, Jean, Mother and Norman came in – and we started making merry all over again.

Wednesday 15

I was taken down to see Mr. Haggarty this morning. He is going to take out my bad teeth under pentothal[25] for me; most probably next Thursday. Kate Schrubshall is also having a tooth out the same day, so we can have a laugh together going down. Father Harrington was hiding behind a screen when I came in – good thing I didn't say anything rude! So we got out the Gin. And he had a drink with us.

Thursday 16

No grading for me again to-day. Most probably I shall be on this bathing grade for a month.

Friday 17

We went down to Kitty Butcher's cubicle this evening for her farewell party. She leaves tomorrow – we shall miss her for she's such a nice girl.

Monday 20

I put on weight again today! I'm now 11.3.7!

---

[23] The ward she was on. I still have it and it is indeed beautiful.

[24] Book by Marguerite Hamilton, published in 1955.

[25] Sodium Pentothal, a rapid-onset short-acting barbiturate general anesthetic. Bet you're glad you know that aren't you?

Thursday 23

Teeth out today, what a performance! They dressed me in a white op. gown, long op. socks and tied my hair up in a white bandana handkerchief. (Katie Schrubshell underwent the same treatment) then I was given a pre-med and after that felt so full of the 'joys of Spring' I could have jumped about. I did get out of bed to show Mary how I looked in my get up, but couldn't do anything more daring as Dt. Johnson was in the office. When he came in to me – just before I 'went down' – he told me I looked glamorous! – in that get up I can well believe it! Then he gave me one walk - to celebrate having my teeth out! The stretcher bearers then carried me down on to a trolley, and pushed me into the theatre wagon next to Kate. We looked exactly like a pair of stiffs ready for the morgue! Being covered up to the chins with blankets and sheets. Anyhow we (felt) nothing once upon the op. table – the pentothal is truly wonderful, no after effects even. In fact, when Mother came in this evening she couldn't believe I'd had them out.

Monday 27

Although I thought I should lose weight this week on account of having my teeth out, I did in fact, gain a few ounces; I'm now 11.3.12.

Tuesday 28

The Diomycin is beginning to play me up again! I feel terribly dizzy, and vague once again.

Figure 20 Art competition comments card, 1956.

Figure 21

September
Rather dull with above average temperatures and near normal rainfall

Monday 3
My weight is up to 11.4.2 now! I do hope I am not going to pile up fat again.

Thursday 6
Dr. J. gave me two walks to-day, and that also means I can now wash at the sink in the morning – hurrah! The docs. mentioned my weight – so maybe I shall be dieted again.

Friday 7
It was heavenly to have a good 'do' at the basin this morning.

Monday 10
Weight was down to-day – 11.3.1

Tuesday 11
Dr. Greenburg took me off Diomycin to-day.

Thursday 13
Dr. Johnson told me my x-ray was going well. But I now have tonsillitis! Sister arranged for me to go down to see Miss Hall the throat specialist and she told me I have tonsillitis. I've to go down to her again in 3 weeks time. No wonder Dr. J. told me I was a complicated case!

Monday 17
Weight was the same today as last week. 11.3.1

Wednesday 19
No diary entry but a letter…

Father John D. Harrington
V
Miss Iris Edgar and Miss Mary Kielthy

I father John D. Harrington, assistant curate of St. John Vianney Church and Roman Catholic Padre to St. Ann's Hospital, N.15, do hereby make public apology to the above-mentioned patients residing in x cubicle, N.1 ward of the said hospital, having made false accusation against these irreproachable unfortunates, declaring at approximately 6.p.m. on the 16 September 1956 that they did wilfully and with malice aforethought hide my bicycle clips during my visit to them on 15 September 1956.

I hereby testify that I did falsely accuse the aforesaid patients and desire to make public apology to Miss I. Edgar and Miss M. Kielthy.

I also declare that the recipients of this apology possess spotless impeccable characters.

I don't think this was intended seriously by Father Harrington[26].

Saturday 22
Bee came to see me this evening – quite unexpectedly. It was lovely to have her here.

Figure 21 Letter extract, 1956.

---

[26] Born in Paddington, London, he was ordained in May 1956 in Westminster Cathedral. His position of assistant curate of St. John Vianney in South Tottenham and padre to St. Ann's was his first appointment. He later went to the USA where he died in 2007. He was noted for his dry sense of humour

Figure 22

November
Very dry and rather cold with above average sunshine

Wednesday 7

It has been quite an ordinary quiet day to-day – we've not 'Gooned' about because a new very ill patient came in this morning. Mother came this afternoon, but only for about ½ hr. as she was going to a reception for a retiring member of the W.V.S.[27]

I went to have another tooth filled this morning – it was very quiet down in the waiting room with Michael not there. Margaret is still so miserable! Wait until Mary knows who I have in with me!

Thursday 22

I had my tonsils out today, at 10 o'clock and feel like nothing on earth now. Joan and Michael came in this afternoon for a few minutes, but of course couldn't stay.

Friday 23

I've had lots of visitors today. Joan and Michael came to tea, Father Harrington called in, and Fred wrote himself out an admission card which said "Admit one." Sister has been awfully good to me, letting all my friends come in.

Saturday 24

Today, I feel much better. I'm still having folks in to see me, and don't really mind being back on strict bed (rest) again – in fact Dr. Mitchell gave me one walk today.

---

[27] The Women's Voluntary Service which became the Women's Royal Voluntary Service WRVS and then the Royal Voluntary Service, is a voluntary organisation concerned with helping people in need in the UK. It was founded in 1938 to recruit women into the Air Raid Precautions (ARP) services to help in the event of a War.

Sunday 25

It seemed very strange today not to be going down to meet visitors!
Margaret is noticeably brighter – in fact I quite enjoy her company at times.

Figure 22 Iris, front room, Dorset Road circa 1957.

1957

'Now she had me to add to her repertoire of terrible stories'

The Mitchley Waltz

Figure 23

Chapter 14
An Introduction to 1957

The year started with the resignation of the Prime Minister Anthony Eden, due to ill health. On 10 January Harold Macmillan took his place. In July he told the nation it had *'never had it so good.'* Indeed, prosperity and growth, albeit uneven, was around the corner and during his six years in office average living standards steadily rose.

In a technological leap that defied their sleepy Norfolk backwater image Norwich City Council installed a computer, the first local authority to do so.

The East Midlands was gently rocked by an earthquake of 5.3 magnitude, and in the world of television an equally important seismic event occurred when the so called 'Toddlers Truce' ended. Up until February 1957 television broadcasting was paused between 18:00 and 19:00 every weekday so toddlers could be put to bed. The BBC received six telephone calls complaining about the change. The slot was filled on weekdays by the news, on Saturdays by music in the form of the Six-Five Special, and on Sunday the BBC remained off air between 18:00 and 19:00 until Songs of Praise was introduced in 1961.

In May petrol rationing following the Suez Crisis finally ended and drivers could fill up the tanks of their cars for the princely sum of 27p a gallon.

The Medical Research Council revealed that they had found evidence to support a link between smoking and lung cancer, although reliable evidence had been emerging from the 1940s onwards.

An influenza pandemic reached our shores, having already claimed thousands of lives on its way. A vaccine was introduced four months later which arrested its spread, but it still claimed around 33,000 lives between 1957 and 1958.

Lonnie Donegan led the rock n' roll lifestyle to the full by appearing as Wishee Washee in pantomime, a role he was to repeat the following year, as we'll discover later.

John Lennon and Paul McCartney met at a fête at St. Peter's Church in Liverpool. Having both bought Lonnie Donegan's Rock Island Line in 1956, they bonded over a shared love of skiffle.

Lennon's group, The Quarrymen, played at the fete. The Cavern Club opened its doors in Matthew Street, where The Quarrymen later performed, before becoming The Beatles.

Public transport was in the news for the wrong reasons in 1957. In June, a bus mowed down a queue of people at a bus stop, killing eight of them. Later in the year a flying boat en-route from Southampton to Las Palmas suffered engine failure and ploughed into a disused chalk pit on the Isle of Wight, claiming forty-five lives and injuring thirteen.

Rail travel was not necessarily any safer. On a foggy December night an electric train to Hayes stopped at a signal approaching Lewisham, and the steam train following behind on its way to Ramsgate crashed into it. The accident happened under a bridge, which collapsed onto the Ramsgate train. Ninety people were killed and one hundred and seventy-three injured.

In a happier, if somewhat dated, event, the Lyceum Ballroom in London hosted the Miss World competition. The organisers struggled as the various contestants went down with the flu, but eventually Marita Lindahl from Finland won. Miss Egypt, Zubaida Tharwat, did not attend in protest at Britain's involvement in the Suez Crisis.

At the cinema you could see David Lean's Academy Award-winning film, The Bridge on the River Kwai. It won seven Academy Awards including best film, best director, best actor for Alec Guinness and best adapted screenplay for Pierre Boulle, who wrote the original 1952 book but had nothing to do with the screen adaptation. Carl Foreman and Michael Wilson, the actual screenwriters, had to write from the UK in secret because they were on the 'Hollywood blacklist' of artists and writers accused of 'un-American' activities. These were generally people who were considered to have Communist sympathies. By 1957 the blacklist was being openly challenged by people such as Alfred Hitchcock, who hired blacklisted actor Norman Lloyd as a producer on his 'Alfred Hitchcock Presents' series.

If you fancied going to see something less likely to trouble the Academy Award judges, Jailhouse Rock starring Elvis Presley was also released in

1957.

At the 71st Wimbledon tennis championships Jimmy Tattersall defeated Ivo Ribeiro of Brazil in the boys' singles final, the only British winner that year.

In Ward N1 of St. Ann's General Hospital, Tottenham, Miss Iris Edgar was to wake up in 1957 to a cold and frosty day and the prospect of spending more time in hospital. On the positive side, she had her friend Mary Kielthy as company and had a very festive Christmas to look back on.

Figure 23 Iris, back garden, Dorset Road 1957.

Figure 24

Chapter 15
Holidays

I can find no trace of Iris' diary for 1957, but two pieces of her memorabilia and one of my fathers did survive from that year.

The first of Iris' is a photo album which records a holiday in Broadstairs in Kent, another holiday or day trip to Margate, various outings and a few odd shots of Norman, Mable and Penny walking in a park. Everyone looks slightly on edge, as if they have been ordered to act natural or else!

The second record is her account of Christmases in 1955 and 1956. It is a peculiar piece, tucked away in with her other papers but written around 1977. It is typed on the back of some scrap paper that lists members of the Essex Youth Orchestra in concert at the Snape Maltings Concert Hall[28] on Sunday 18th September 1977, so I am assuming it's from around then.

I do not know why she wrote it or felt the need to hold on to it.

It does though confirm that she stayed in hospital into 1957. This seems like an appropriate place to include it.

My tale takes us on to the early 1950s. I was diagnosed as having pulmonary tuberculosis and, in those days, cures took a lot longer than they do today.

It was about a week after Christmas 1955 that I was first sent to the Chest Clinic and told that I was to go home to bed and rest. My mother told her neighbour next day and being a very morbid lady anyway she revelled in the news. Her main conversation was who had died and had bad births and cancer.

Now she had me to add to her repertoire of terrible stories. She called in every day to see how I was but was much too nervous of catching the 'bug' to come upstairs to see me. On the odd occasion that she did come up she stood in the doorway or sat right by the open window no matter how cold.

---

[28] My Father by this time, was the accountant for the Aldeburgh Festival Foundation who owned and ran the concert hall.

So when the following Xmas came round and I was still ill imagine my surprise when she called on Xmas eve and invited my mother and myself to spend Xmas day with her and her family.

Knowing how she felt we refused the invitation but she was very upset that we turned her invite down – so as I was then grading up to 6 hrs. a day we agreed to visit her for Xmas tea.

Well we were made welcome; I took my own cutlery and crockery with me but she would have none of it. I sat back that evening while the festivities went on around me and wondered what it is about Xmas that made me acceptable and non-contagious at that time.

There is something about Xmas that brings out the best in people. Friends were marvellous. I had cards and presents from people that I didn't even know very well.

It can also bring out reminiscence. My grandmother was also a lady of very morbid tastes. Whenever she came to see me she would gaze at me and shake her head as though I was wasting away – in fact I was putting on weight so fast through inactivity that the Drs. at the chest clinic made me diet.

But on that boxing day Grandmother came. She sat and talked of nothing else but Christmases past when she had nursed her sister and then her cousin with T.B.

Of course they had both died and it was quite obvious that she thought that this particular Xmas was going to be history repeating itself. Our neighbour was afraid of catching the 'bug' again once Xmas was over.

The following Xmas I was in hospital. I was in a double room with a very lively companion. I had gone into hospital in April 1956 and when the build up to Xmas '56 began the atmosphere in the ward was wonderful. From our room we could hear the nurses practising carols in the chapel.

We were both up for a number of hours each day so we decorated our room and the big ward was lovely with a large tree and masses of decorations.

There was a sad side to this Xmas though. Some patients had not seen their children for a very long time, years even. Some had lost their husbands to other women who were available and not ill and while during the year these patients were sad but over it in a short time as Xmas approached there were several very low spirited women obviously thinking about happier days.

Stevie's Xmas present to Mary[29] was cleaning her teeth and me cutting her hair.

Iris Canham
Circa 1977

Figure 24 Margate 1957.

---

[29] Mary was the other patient sharing the room with Iris. Stevie may have been another patient, a relative or friend of Mary's.

Figure 25

Chapter 16
Discovering the Modern Boy

The mid to late 1950s witnessed many changes to the way we lived and worked. One of the most influential, and to many threatening, was the rise of the teenager.

Fashion conscious and full of youthful exuberance and raging hormones, they adopted their own distinct identities, often defined by the music they listened to.

One of the most visible of the new trend setters were the Teddy Boys, who were often presented by the press as the perpetrators of violence and delinquency. At first glance rising crime figures appeared to support this notion, but this was largely a statistical phenomenon produced by new approaches to policing and changes in the collation of crime data.[30]

We can get a small first-hand glimpse into the mind of the post-war adult population witnessing the rise of the teenager from a Boys Brigade display that my father wrote in 1957 called The Modern Boy.

In his handwriting, he carefully scripted a series of vignettes:

Up to now you have been seeing what the present day boy does at BB.

In our next item 'the Modern Boy' we are going to show you what the boys do in their spare time, but first let us have a look at the boys of previous reigns.

There follow examples from the Victorian (violin), Edwardian (hoop and stick) and George V (keystone cops style skit) eras, before arriving at

---

[30] Bill Osgerby - author and professor with a focus on modern American and British media and cultural history writing for The Subculture Network and reproduced at museumofyouthculture.com. I don't just make this up you know!

the Elizabethan era of 'The Modern Boy' with a skiffle band.

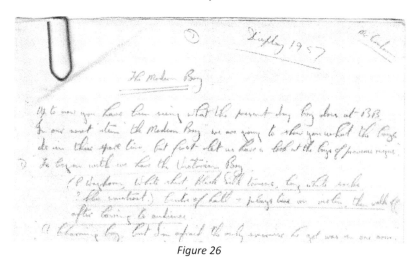

Figure 26

As the band take their curtain call the compere's script reads:

'It seems to me they (the modern boy) get plenty of exercise, except possibly in the head, but its harmless and amuses the girls so perhaps the modern boy is an improvement on the boys of previous reigns.'

Tolerated, indulged and lightly patronised perhaps, but there was also a recognition that the 'modern boy' was injecting some colour and life into the world.

Little did my father know as he sat and wrote that show that the following year his world was to change for ever…

Figure 25 Norman, front room, Dorset Road, 1957.
Figure 26 Extract from The Modern Boy, 1957.

The Mitchley Waltz

1958

Enter the dreaming tortoise...

The Mitchley Waltz

Figure 27

Chapter 17
An Introduction to 1958

As the first light of the new year of 1958 broke through it fell on a London in transition.

The Second World War had been over for more than a decade, but many streets still had gaps where houses had been bombed, and many families were still struggling in a faltering economy.

Smog, a potentially lethal mix of coal smoke and sulphur dioxide remained an occasional menace despite the introduction of the Clean Air Act in 1956. In 1957 smoke and carbon monoxide levels were equal to the 'Great Smog' of 1952, which claimed an estimated 12,000 lives and prompted the Act.

Smoke from chimneys wasn't banned in London until the following decade.

Rock 'n' Roll had taken off, Teddy Boys grabbed the attention of the press, and Jerry Lee Lewis had his 1958 tour of the UK cut short when it was revealed that the new bride accompanying him was his 13-year-old cousin.

American cinema and popular music influenced fashion and introduced colour and ready to wear clothing into the mainstream. Formal attire was still considered appropriate for an evening at the ballroom, but some formal traditions were coming to an end as the last debutante was presented to the Queen.

The National Health Service celebrated its ten-year anniversary by launching a programme to vaccinate everyone under the age of 15 against polio and diphtheria. Although the vaccine had been available since 1956 this was the first mass vaccination programme. Prior to its introduction polio cases could climb as high as 8,000 in epidemic years, and cases of diphtheria as high as 70,000, leading to 5,000 deaths. This vaccination programme would lead to an immediate and dramatic reduction in both diseases.

Nurse's working hours were reduced to 88 a fortnight, prescription charges were 1 shilling an item (5p) and average life expectancy was just over ten years shorter than today.

The Boeing 707 entered commercial service and heralded the age of the jet liner as it came to dominate the airline business. It was the BOAC Comet however that became the first jet passenger service to cross the Atlantic. Foreign holidays were a real prospect for many for the first time, although most people still headed to coastal resorts in the UK.

The Preston by-pass opened, notable because it was the first stretch of motorway in the UK, the M1 would follow in 1959. Another motoring innovation introduced in 1958 was not so welcome, the parking meter.

The Campaign for Nuclear Disarmament was established, and Britain went into battle with Iceland over fishing rights in the first 'Cod War'.

Grandstand and Blue Peter debuted on our television sets and the State Opening of Parliament was broadcast for the first time. In the cinema the first in the Carry-On series, Carry on Sergeant premiered.

The Darling Buds of May and Paddington Bear made their first appearances in print.

Bolton Wanderers won the F.A. Cup, beating a Manchester United team depleted after eight of the team were among the 44 fatalities of the Munich air disaster earlier in the year.

Housing was being built at record levels, with up to 45 families a week being housed in new builds across the UK. Nevertheless, many people still lived in prefabricated housing, originally built as temporary accommodation to replace housing destroyed by bombs in the War.

Local Authorities were given 'slum clearance' powers, new towns took 'overspill' from cities and high-rise flats appeared on the skyline in ever increasing numbers.

The year 1958 also came to be a pivotal year for race relations in the UK. The generation who came over from the Caribbean on ships like the Empire Windrush shortly after World War 2 were settled and putting down roots. A new generation of citizens were born here to immigrant families, and cities like London found themselves in a state of change as cultures and lifestyles mixed, and sometimes clashed.

Politicians often pandered to racial stereotypes and public mistrust to get elected and inevitably tensions could run high.

One area of friction between the Caribbean population and members of the white working class was Notting Hill, which in August 1958 erupted into rioting, stoked up by extreme right-wing parties like Sir Oswald Mosely's British Union of Fascists.

The following year a Caribbean Carnival was started as a response to the state of race relations in the UK, which was the forerunner of the present-day Notting Hill Carnival.

Author Colin MacInnes wrote his seminal novel Absolute Beginners in 1958, in which he documents the vibrancy of a multi-cultural city finding its feet amid the tensions and clashes of culture.

But despite the troubles and tensions, people still went out to ballrooms, jazz clubs and to the cinema, they went to work, school, church and joined the Boys Brigade and Civil Defence Corps. They shopped, worked, laughed, cried, and they fell in love.

In Tottenham Iris was recovering from TB and was beginning to regain her strength. As she opened her diary to record the events of the first day of what was to be an important year for her…

Figure 27 Donald Canham.

Figure 28

Chapter 18
Full and unabridged Diary 1958

January
Rather mild with below average rainfall and sunshine.

Wednesday 1

Clinic today! There were loads of people there-and a new Radiographer-just to add to the 'joys' of the clinic. Nevertheless Dr. Johnson was his usual kind self. He wasn't so keen on my result this time, but as he said he was seeing some 'weird and wonderful' pictures from the new radiographer – so I'm hoping my actual result was as good as usual. I didn't have the pluck though to ask for permission to dance.

When I got back to work the first thing they did was come and see how I had faired – it was kind of people, and makes one feel grateful.

I am trying my hardest to keep patience with Mrs. Thompson.

Friday 3

We had our final meeting tonight for the Civil Defence Social[31]. Mr

---

[31] The Civil Defence Corp was formed in 1949 to mobilise and take local control of the affected area in the aftermath of a major national emergency, like a Cold War nuclear attack. By March 1956, the Civil Defence Corps had 330,000 personnel. Many of the Corps developed active social clubs too, and Tottenham was no exception.

Lloyd has bought rosettes for the stewards, and a lovely one for me, with an M.C's badge in the centre. Folks arrived very early for the dancing – in fact before we had finished the meeting. They are all terribly keen. Mr Lloyd has asked me if I can carry on with the lessons after the social. I said I would until March (my next clinic check) and probably after that.

Monday 6
Jean and I sung folk songs this evening – I had to take the words down in shorthand before I could sing them, of course. We played the results back on Jean's tape recorder and I must say they are quite good!

Wednesday 8
This afternoon Mother and I went to Burgess's to buy the material for my dress I'm to wear for the social. I also got a rose for my hair, and white gloves.

Then this evening I met Jean at Leicester Square Station from where we made our way to Chiswick to see Lonnie Donnegan (sic) as Whishee Washee in Aladdin. It was a very good show. I have a very bad foot -my toe is swelling and looks awful – I hope its O.K. for Saturday.

Friday 10
This evening we were a large crowd at the C.D. (Civil Defence) to put up the decorations for tomorrow evening. Then the dancing carried on as usual, and we went over the programme for tomorrow. I do hope everything goes off fine.

Saturday 11
The day itself when I am M.C. for the first time! I have asked God to be with me – and I don't feel nervous. I wore my new dress -and very nice it looks too. Miss Evans and Mrs Lloyd took me round to meet the people who were there earliest and then I met the Pianist (Mrs Knowles) and Mrs Daniels (the accordionist). Mrs Moffat performed her mimes, and there were other members of the Harringay Dramatic Society who put monologues over – however there were far too many of these acts, and most of the audience wished them fewer.

Anyway, I was congratulated very warmly afterwards by a good many folks and the musicians told me they "enjoyed working with someone who knew what they were doing"! Very gratifying! Before the evening began Mr. Lloyd took me upstairs to his office – together with the Committee – and they presented me with a lovely box of chocolates.

Jean and Mary enjoyed themselves.

Laurie Hookins, whom I asked some time ago to lead the dances with me, was petrified ever since I asked him, and decided to help behind the bar with Mr. Salisbury[32]. Anyhow next time I shall ask Mr. Cannon (sic) to help – I danced twice with him during the evening - and I have a feeling he would be only too pleased to help me![33]

Monday 13

Jean brought her guitar with her this evening, and once more we sung folksongs. I love our musical evenings.

Wednesday 14

I had a letter of thanks from Mr. Lloyd today – he seems very pleased with our efforts at the social.

Thursday 15

We have hardly any work, and today I've been doing my French. This evening we were fairly busy giving out the R.S.A certificates.[34]

Friday 16

Still doing my French at work – then Mr. Rose gave me some typing.

6W class went very well this evening – we had nearly 40 people there – Mr Lloyd was thrilled to bits. Before we began dancing those of us who were early finished up the drink from last Saturday. I started them on the Lancers tonight. Laurie was much better – he seems really relieved now that the social is over, and I shall not have to ask him to partner me when leading off. One could truly sense his relief. What a strange fellow!

Saturday 17

I had a letter from the Fosters this morning – they would like me to go and see them. It is nice to think that people still like to see one after a long time[35].

Figure 28 Extract of set list, Saturday 11 January 1958.

---

[32] Laurie Hookins won a spot prize with Mrs. Gascoigne for the Progressive Barn Dance - the cad!
[33] My father enters our story as a bit player in the drama of the C.D. social club, who got his big break thanks to the cowardice of Laurie Hookins. I find it endearing that she misspelt his name.
[34] RSA is the Royal Society of Arts exam board, now part of Oxford, Cambridge & RSA Examinations.
[35] The Fosters from Leconfield, IOW. It is a masterpiece in brevity. There is no date on it, but it is headed Wed. and signed off 'nearly 12 O'clock'.

Figure 29

March

Cold and rather dry with above average sunshine

Friday 14

This afternoon I went to Betty's for my lessons – I think I am getting on quite well. I was late getting my bus home, and so was late in arriving at the C.D. headquarters.

My class went well again – I taught the "Embassy Blues". Mr Cannons (sic) has agreed to lead-off with me at the next social (or dance, whichever Mr. Lloyd agrees to). He is beginning to lead off now all the classes, and is doing very well. He told me this evening that Linda was very struck with me last week – he said "you are her hero – if a woman can be called a hero, or perhaps I should say idol – that's more like her reaction to you". Very complimentary from a child!

Wednesday 19

This evening I met Jean from work at 6. O'clock and we caught the 6.38 p.m. from Victoria to Crawley. What a journey! We didn't get home to the Elliotts until 7.45. How Jean can do that every day I do not know.

Thursday 20

This morning I went to Crawley Town Shopping Centre with Mrs. E. and Jean. It was bitterly cold, but in spite of that I thoroughly enjoyed my first glimpse of a "New Town". The shops are set under arcades – and the roads very wide apart. However the rows and rows of council houses do not really appeal to me, although they are spacious and well planned.

Instead of going for our planned walk in the woods this afternoon we stayed in and drew, listened to records and sang to Jean's guitar. It snowed quite a lot.

Friday 21

Home again today. We caught the 9 o'clock train from Crawley and arrived in Victoria Station at ¼ past ten. What a journey to do each day! But Jean doesn't mind it.

This afternoon I caught the early bus to Betty's. We flogged away at the waltz. Then this evening I plugged away at it with my own class.

Saturday 22

Mrs Callier told us this morning that Vera Thomas has to go into hospital under observation for T.B. – poor Vera[36]. I hope she will be able to accept it.

Sunday 23

I turned my room out this morning – and then this afternoon finished Mother's portrait. I'm very pleased with it.

Thursday 27

What a strange post for me this morning! A letter from Mortons, containing a lot of scandal about Betty. Happening to know Betty's side of those stories I feel very cross at people gossiping in such a way. Mrs. M. tells me that the Cuttings are willing to help me with my dancing – little do they know that Betty is putting me through for my letters![37] I shall have to tell people soon though that I am dancing again, because when I'm qualified I shall not stay in the background!

There was also a letter from Bernard! He is enquiring after my health and tells me he has had a promotion in his job – perhaps he tells me this as an incentive! I wonder. Fancy writing to me after all this time. However, I shall reply, but not just yet.

I met mother for lunch today in Burgesses. She was with Mrs Vince, Miss Morris, Mrs Burns and her brother-in-law. They are on a C.D. exercise. I sat with Mr. Burns – he has such a funny brogue! I cannot understand what he says. Anyway he paid for the meal and a drink, then drove us back (them to Mitchley Road[38], me to the college).

It was very quiet at work this evening.

---

[36] Aside from the obvious worry of a potentially life altering diagnosis faced by poor Vera, TB still carried a stigma in 1958. Although it had been known to be an infectious disease since the end of the 1800s, even in 1950 55% of the population who answered in a survey about public attitudes towards tuberculosis believed it to be hereditary. A TB diagnosis could still result in loss of friends and employment.

[37] International Dance Teacher Association (IDTA) exam that would be the path to becoming a qualified dance teacher.

[38] Mitchley Road Mission Halls in Mitchley Road. Built in 1910 as a second small church and Sunday School for the Anglican Church of St Mary the Virgin, Tottenham. It was the local headquarters of the Civil Defence and used as the venue for their socials.

Friday 28

Mr. Lloyd and Miss Evans asked me this evening if I would put on a show on the 18th April at the presentation of first aid certs. (Certificates). I said of course I should, and chose a team of my 'best' dancers. Only for couples: Mr White and Miss Rivetts, Mother and Mr. Woods, Stan and Mrs White, Mr Canham and I.

They all fell in line at once when I asked them to do it for me - in fact poor Mr Canham was absent when the arrangements were being made; and when he came in I told him he was my 'volunteered' partner.[39] He willingly agreed – I was very pleased. Miss Rivetts has offered the loan of her flat for a meeting of my team on the Tuesday after Easter – we shall have loads of work to do before they are ready. The women I think will wear black skirts and white blouses, the men dark suits – but everything is very much in the air at present.

Saturday 29

Have been perming my hair this afternoon. Hope it turns out O.K. Have just heard on the news that a widow of 65 who killed 3 husbands and her lover has been sentenced to death. I pray she will be reprieved – how barbaric it seems to kill someone by hanging. Who are we to judge![40]

Sunday 30

My hair has turned out extremely good – with God's help. Edna and Connie came this evening. Edna spent most of her visit complaining of her mother! Poor Edna, she certainly has a lot to put up with – her Mother always has been possessive. I felt guilty when they were going – we were teasing Mother about "boy friends" and Connie said – "you will have to go Old Time Dancing to find a real smasher! – little do they know that we go O.T.D[41] again. Somehow though I just cannot be bothered to tell them.

Figure 29 Envelope from Civil Defence, 1958.

---

[39]Some may say that was the story of his life once he had met my mother.
[40] Mary Wilson, the 'Merry Widow of Windy Nook' as she became known, murdered two of her husbands with beetle poison and probably all four of them. She came to the attention of the police because of her sense of humour - she had joked at her last wedding reception that left-over sandwiches would be fresh enough to use at the next funeral, and then asked the undertaker for a trade discount. mother's prayers were answered when her sentence was commuted to life imprisonment.
[41] Old time dancing

Figure 30

April
Rather wet with near normal temperatures and sunshine

Saturday 5

Mother and I met Mr. and Mrs. White at South Tot. Station just in time to catch the 7 O'clock train. We spent a most enjoyable evening at Leyton Town Hall[42]. Betty saved our seats right in front of the band with her and Bill. I expected the fellow from Clacton to be partnering her but Bill it was! He looks very good of course in his tails. I had a few dances with him – and how grand it is to once again dance with someone that can dance![43]. Maisie and Jimmy, Mrs Taylor and of all people George Smith came and spoke to me – G.S. told me he still sees Edna and Connie – so they will no doubt hear of my dancing at Leyton Town Hall!! The Whites and Mother enjoyed themselves tremendously – they are more keen than ever. Ron Kempsall came – he waited outside for an hour for us to arrive – Bill asked me during the evening if anymore friends of mine were coming – I of course said no as it was getting late – however Bill asked the doorman to send him up – he had eventually asked for us 'on the door'. What a freak! Betty had a great crowd at Leyton – really a room full of excellent dancers. She has done very

---

[42] According to it's website "Leyton Great Hall is the jewel in the crown of the Legacy Business Centre in Leyton, E10". I don't know how many venues compete for this auspicious title, but it does look like a rather marvellous, fully restored Art Nouveau venue. It must have been a splendid sight with dancers twirling under the lights in the great hall.

[43] A glimpse of Iris as I knew her. She would always aim to be the best she could at dancing and expected no less of anyone else. I seldom witnessed her dancing for pleasure rather than teaching, but I can imagine that a good partner was a real treat.

well! We got home at about 12.30 very tired of course, but I must say I wasn't as tired as I thought I should be.

Figure 30 Iris, 1958.

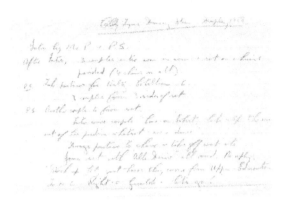

Figure 31

May

Cold and dry with near average sunshine

Saturday 31

This evening Mother and I went with Mr. Canham to the B.B. (Boys Brigade)[44] display – it was very good – and some items were extremely funny. We were in V.I.P. seats with Linda and Mr. C's sister Jean. Mr. and Mrs. White were there too, but not sitting with us; we saw them for a few moments before and after the display. I was pleased with the dancing item I had helped the boys with – they all came over to me and thanked me again – they're a grand crowd! I was introduced to the Captain, who promptly whisked me out to the little hall for a cup of tea – then Jean and Mother were brought out for one. Mother and I went home to Mr. Canham's flat for a cup of tea after the show. On the way home Mother told me that while I was in Linda's room he told her that Linda wants me for her "Mother". According to my Mother he is rather keen too. He is extremely nice, and I don't know what I shall feel about things later on; but at the moment I still feel I should be an awful burden on anyone. And then there is my dancing – I feel that it is a gift I should use, and that my health has been maintained well enough to get permission from Dr. Johnson to dance so that I can use it.

Figure 31 Extract, Boys Brigade display by Don.

---

[44] My father was a stalwart of the Boys Brigade. He was the band instructor (bugle and drums marching band), for the 3rd Tottenham Company. He became an Officer in the company on 28th January 1947. Apart from the band, he took part in gymnastic displays, parades, he led camping trips and helped organise their shows and entertainment.

I have his collection of Class Roll Books for band practice and can see that for the year 1958/59 there were 18 regular band members, three trainee buglers, and a waiting list. I'm sure that you are keen to know that K. Elvin and P. Jones worked out okay as buglers, but K Harris sadly didn't make the grade.

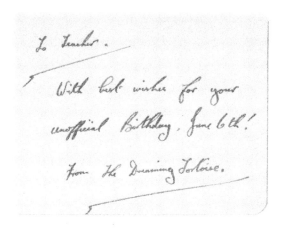

Figure 32

June
Very wet, dull and rather cool

Sunday 1

Haven't done a lot today! I painted this afternoon, and brushed Penny – but I feel rested.

Wednesday 4

Tony rang me this morning to remind me of our date this evening. I was hoping he had forgotten. Even Betty thinks it is a funny set up! I met him at Turnpike Lane[45] (don't want him to know where I live). Norman ran me to the station and said he would meet me at about 11! Of course he didn't know who I was going out with. Anyway we drove out to Potters Bar and had a drink, then drove through the lanes of Hertfordshire home. The evening was not so bad as I thought it would be, but Tony is, I realize, more interested in me than I like. He told me that he had married in America and brought his wife back here. He then had invalid parents, and as his wife wished to return to her own country and he would not leave his parents, she divorced him! It was a very 'pretty' little sob story; and then he told me that I would make him a good companion.[46] I couldn't bear it!

Then, serve me right, we arrived at Turnpike Lane and I said "good I can meet Norman on his way". I dived home but Norman came out early!

---

[45] Turnpike Lane was the site of a turnpike used to collect tolls from travellers from 1739 to 1872 when the turnpike system was abolished. In 1958 it was a major traffic crossroads, underground station and bus depot.
[46] To me that sounds more like a business relationship or an advertisement from The Lady than passion.

So I took Penny and we found Norman waiting for us by the coffee stall, surrounded by Irishmen admiring the car. I was all-in when I got home and had a huge supper of chips and corned beef and spam.

Thursday 5

I rang Betty to tell her about last evening, but didn't get far as Mr. Rose came in and I had to cut our call short. Anyway I can give her all the 'gen' on Wednesday. I worked out the Crinoline Gavotte ready to put on tomorrow evening. Also I planned out my letter in answer to Bernard's – I've had that for about 3 months! My answer will be only very brief and to the point – no frills – and I can only hope to finish his feelings for me.

Friday 6

I've not had much to do at work to-day. Blanche and Mr. B take their exam. on Monday and Tuesday. I do hope they cope well – particularly Blanche. They're going to find it a bit hard getting there with the bus strike still going on[47]. I wonder when it will end – all the meetings so far have ended in deadlock.

When I arrived home from work this evening there was a parcel for me. It was a box of chocolates from Don Canham[48] "for my unofficial birthday" - June 6th! (He dreamed once that my birthday was then)[49]. Then he asked me this evening if I'd go with him, Pam and Gerry, Dennis (G's brother) and his cousin Joan to the Salon Bal, tomorrow evening. I Agreed! Norman ran a crowd of his home tonight.

Saturday 7

Well I certainly had a lovely time this evening. Don called for me, then we met the others at Belmont Road (Dennis has a car – we drove straight to a little pub in Harringay and had a drink, then got to the dance at about ¼ past 9. (ready for a cup of tea!) The Salon Bal has been altered quite a bit, the band is now downstairs in one corner, and the balcony is used as a buffett. (Sic) We had a lovely time then after the dance we bought fish and chips and all went back to Don's and ate fish and chips and drank Dubonnett! (Sic) I got home at 1 O'clock. But I had a grand evening.

Monday 30

I rang Jean this morning to let her know I couldn't meet her as arranged on Wed. because of the Gov. Body meeting. When I asked how Suzie was

---

[47] The bus strike had been ongoing since May 5 and would not end until June 20. It saw the complete shutdown of all Central and Country route services,

[48] "To teacher, with best wishes for your unofficial birthday, June 6th! From the dreaming Tortoise".

[49] When I started reading her diary, I used a small card I found inside as a bookmark. When I reached June 6, I looked again at the card and realised I was using the card from that very box of chocolates from over 60 years ago!

she said "She died this morning". She wasn't even ill again – just died! Perhaps she had a heart attack after all she has been through. I couldn't ask much about it at so early a stage, so must try and find out more when I see Jean next week.[50]

Figure 32 The Dreaming Tortoise 'birthday' card.

---

[50] Suzie's death seems to have been recorded in rather matter of fact terms, maybe because of the nature of recording a diary and perhaps having lived through the War and seeing TB patients pass away, indeed having been close to death herself, mother became a little immune to it.

Figure 33

July

Above average sunshine, below normal temperatures and near average rainfall.

Tuesday 1

Miss Lane asked me first thing this morning about an application form for a teaching post that she cannot find. I think she felt that I had it – but it was with Mr. Smith all the time! She and Mr. Roe don't seem to quite know what they are doing lately. We had a good laugh this afternoon when there were four applicants being interviewed for teaching posts. We all had to make a note of their names – and Blanche had to take them into Mr. Roe in alphabetical order. Miss Lane having told her exactly what to do, and even what to say! A good job we can laugh over the Tec. College or all our self – confidence would be sapped. The way Peggy's has been.

The weather today has been atrocious again – why don't we ever have any sun?

That is all that she recorded for July, but tucked into her diary was the above letter dated July 24 from Mr Lloyd, the Civil Defence Officer of Tottenham Sub Division who states that he was 'very pleased to hear of the progress that you are making with the "Mitchley Waltz". This is the first time that its mentioned, so I like to think that my parents spent time together during July working on it.

Figure 33 Letter re The Mitchley Waltz.

Figure 34

August
Very dull and wet with below average temperatures.

Monday 4

Holiday Monday – but we spent it very quietly at home. I did a bit of painting and went once again over my dances for Wednesday night.

After breakfast this morning I plucked up courage and told Mother how I'd forgotten my scripts yesterday and had to come back for them on our way home from Don's parents to his home. She only moaned a little – primarily this time because the place was not tidy! But then I told her about the games we had with Linda and she was laughing and alright. I don't know why I'm nervous to tell her about bringing people home, but there it is - I am! Particularly at present, after her telling me on Friday that she doesn't like Don calling as she feels ashamed to face the neighbours as I have had so many men friends! I suppose things will work themselves out.

Wednesday 6

I asked Miss Lane for the afternoon off today, and when I did get home I slept all afternoon! But I was glad of a sleep! We had a lovely time at the Majestic – and I did very well with my demonstrating. Harold is very patient, and he was extremely pleased with me. Don and Mother had a grand time; I was disappointed about Norman – he didn't have time to change or shave so sat in the car all the time – he read and had a talk with the car park attendant. Don went out to see him in the interval. Although all went so well, really everyone else carried me along – even Miss Lane by letting me have the afternoon off. My Mother dressed me beautifully in pink flowered nylon – and Don let me practise my dances on him.

Coming home Don told me how everyone was watching me, particularly in the Veletta, in an admiring way. I feel very pleased and hope Betty will be. The evening was such a success that Harold thinks they may be able to hold a 'band night' every Wednesday. The owners of the Majestic were thrilled to bits.

Thursday 7

I was very tired today but pleased with myself. I got lost this evening on my way to the Loughton Club. Daft-like I walked back and forth in front of the hall before going in to see if it was the place. Anyway Harold was pleased with me again and that is all that matters.

I had a letter from Jean this morning asking me to meet her next Wed. evening – she is still going out with Frank the West Indian! Her parents will be so upset[51] – but I hope I can help.

Friday 8

After the dance this evening we walked home with Don. When we left the others at the bottom of Scales Road, Mother went walking off with Miss Rivett, and the Hollands. I suggested we hide from her and Don and I hid behind a wall. Then along came Mother to find us – she was furious! She thought we had been "snogging". It was No (Sic) use arguing with her, but why does she adopt this attitude. Sometimes I wonder if it's worth having a friend of the opposite sex, but then what would I do about my dancing. What is so ludicrous, is the fact that a more detached pair it would be difficult to find. Don goes away for a week tomorrow, so perhaps Mother might forget the incident in the meantime.

Tuesday 12

We have had strange weather today – storms and hot sun – alternatively with each other. I've been fairly busy these last two days at work – but this afternoon I began to get clear again. I tried on my blue and white two-piece this evening, and must have lost weight for it's a perfect fit again. Then my grey dancing dress! How long it seems now. Mother shortened it this evening and I shall wear it for my classes this week. Mother gave me her crystal beads! I'm so thrilled because they have always been a favourite with me. Norman is better again after his two days bilious, and will go to work tomorrow.

---

[51] Well, this is awkward. I don't believe my mother was racist in any way that we'd recognise today – she inherently mistrusted everyone until they had proved themselves to her. Her cynicism was towards the rest of the human race, irrespective of the colour of their skin, politics, religion or sexuality.

Wednesday 13

Majestic with Harold again this evening – and who should walk in but a couple from my old dancing days who know Edna and Connie well! Still they will have to know sometime what I am doing.

Thursday 14

29 Today! I've had a load of cards and some lovely presents. My life seems to be slipping away so fast.

I found my way straight away tonight to the Loughton Club. I really have enjoyed working with Harold over these past two weeks – particularly at the Leyton club – they are such a grand crowd.

Friday 15

I missed Don terribly at the dancing class tonight. Alan fits in very well, but it isn't like having Don around.

Tuesday 19

I went to Don's this evening, and thought he might say something about my Mother's attitude of the other Friday – the last time I saw him. But he didn't mention the episode.

Thursday 21

All day I have been dreading this evening! I'm seeing Edna! Its been busy but nice at work – just Blanche and I in.

It all went off very well at Edna's after all. She didn't mention dancing once although I'm sure she must have heard about my "return to the ballroom". Her new home in the prefab is lovely[52]. Much nicer than I expected in fact. There is every facility for comfort, and of course, compared to a large house as she had before, is easy to cope with. After making a thorough 'tour of inspection' of the new home she told me all about her holiday in Spain. Sounds lovely.

Friday 22

I had my lesson this afternoon and then this evening my class. It was grand having Don back again to help me. We arranged to work tomorrow evening on the Mitchley Waltz – we can give all our time to it as Linda is away.

---

[52] Pre-fabricated (pre-fab) housing was part of the wartime coalition government's plan to alleviate housing shortages after the War. By 1951 when the programme officially ended over 156,000 had been constructed.

Saturday 23

Don and I spent three hours trying to arrange the steps of this waltz properly. We used Dorothy's record player and the Missouri Waltz record and round and round his room we danced[53]. Then at 11 o'clock we relaxed with a cup of tea and Peter Scott on television. I am truly grateful to Don – we have the house all on our own, and I know he admires me, but never once has he made advances. I'm so glad because I think I should have to stop seeing him if he did – hard as it would be – as in all fairness I couldn't be serious with him as much as I like him.

Monday 25

I started my other weeks holiday today – did nothing much but sit in the garden. Anyway the weather is good.

Tuesday 26

I sat in the garden again today, then had a lay down this afternoon and went sound asleep, so sound did I sleep that I didn't wake up until after Don was here at ¼ past six! He only laughed, he's very good tempered with me. After tea we worked on the music for the Mitchley Waltz – its coming on extremely well – I kept filling Don with sherry to give him inspiration.

Wednesday 27

Spent the day in the garden again – then met Jean at 6.30. We had a lovely evening just walking along the Embankment and then sitting opposite Parliament watching the sunset on the river – it was so peaceful. She is still seeing her West Indian friend. They have another dog now – Belinda – a little mongrel dog, and very lovable apparently.

Thursday 28

Don took me to the Radio Show at Earls Court this evening[54]. We traipsed all round looking at the record players – and the one I like is a "Bush". We couldn't find out much about the voltage though so Don is going to find more out about this particular model for me[55]. We came away from the show very tired, and then home to my place for a cup of tea. Then I took Penny home with Don, and we introduced her to Whiskey (Stone's

---

[53] We get the first hint at what the Mitchley Waltz might have sounded like. The Missouri Waltz was based upon an old minstrel song and first published in 1914. It gained popularity in 1939 when Fred Astaire and Ginger Rodgers included it in their film The Story of Vernon and Irene Castle.

[54] The Earls Court Radio Show was in its 25th year in 1958. Products ranged from the everyday, like radios and television sets, to the bizarre, which in 1958 included a TV inside a barrel, that you could pour beer from.

[55] In the late 1950's there was no standardised mains voltage in the UK, because not everywhere was on the national grid. For example, until 1960 the London borough of West Ham ran on Alternating Current and the neighbouring borough ran on Direct Current. A record player exclusively designed for one system wouldn't work on the other.

dog). Although he is very old, and in his ways most senile, our Penny made him frisk-up and even run. His whiskers twitched and his tail wagged – she certainly put new life into him. Eventually we had to return, Penny and I, as he began to bark and as it was late the neighbours would have been none too pleased.

Friday 29

We began to teach the Mitchley waltz this evening – I think it will be quite popular with the class.

Figure 34 Earls Court Radio Show programme, 1958.

Figure 35

September

Very wet and rather warm with slightly above average sunshine.

Tuesday 2

This evening I met Don and Linda in the park with Penny. Then Linda and I took Penny home while Don went back to his place to prepare some drinks. I gave Linda some seedlings at long last! Then I took Linda home and stayed with Don, just talking and talking, until quite late.

Tuesday 9

I had my lesson this evening at 6.30, and although I was a bit tired coped quite well. Betty is quite pleased with me.

Wednesday 10

Jean and I went for a trip up the river this evening. First they took us to Greenwich and then turn-about to Battersea. It was a very pretty trip – it was dark most of the time and especially at Battersea with all the lights of the pleasure gardens reflecting on the water. We thoroughly enjoyed ourselves.[56]

---

[56] Battersea Pleasure Gardens had been the site of the 1951 Festival of Britain, which included a pavilion with space for 400 couples on the dance floor and 700 spectators, all under a vast central canopy. In 1958 the gardens were not on the same scale but many of the 'dressings' from the festival remained, like the strings of lights on the Thames embankment, and it hosted regular fun fairs.

Thursday 11

My first evening on duty at work – this session that is. Olive, Mr. Davis, Miss Cox and I – only 33 enrolments! Mr. Davis didn't even write a receipt.

Friday 12

Don's birthday! I bought him a half bottle of sherry – but got 'wagged' when I gave it to him! Still I think he was pleased. Linda came to the class this evening. The folks are getting on very well with the Mitchley – and the music is complete.

Saturday 13

I went to Don's Mother for tea, then we played in the garden with Linda and Pete at ball until we could see no more, then came home to Don's.

Tuesday 16

Don took me to see "My Fair Lady". It was wonderful! He's very nice to go out with. On the way home he remarked that it was the first time he had taken me out entirely on our own. I gave a non-committal answer so as not to prolong a conversation in any way connected with our two-selves. I find I have to well and truly steel myself against softening towards Don.[57]

Thursday 18

I was on enrolment duty again this evening and we were quite busy – not a bit like last week.

Friday 19

This may be Don's last full evening at the classes, as his Boys Brigade duties start again next week. I shall miss him, but Alan, I know, will step into the breach.

Saturday 20

Norman took Mrs. White, Stan, Alan, Don, Mother and me over to Claybury this evening for Betty's dance. It was a good-time once again. Tony Fisher[58] came down at the end of the evening and tried to get me to one side, but I clung onto Don's arm (he wondered what had come over me). Anyway Tony took the hint which is all that matters. During the evening several of the Loughton crowd came over to ask me to go to their monthly dance next Sat. I don't know what I shall do, as Don and I really

---

[57] My Fair Lady starred Julie Andrews and Stanley Holloway. It should have also featured Rex Harrison but at this performance the part of Henry Higgins was played by Charles Stapley. Charles was known for two things, one was playing Ted Hope in the long running soap Crossroads, the other for a feud played out in the press with his stepdaughter Heather Mills McCartney.

[58] Tony Fisher was a trumpeter with the Ken Mackintosh band in 1958.

want to get down to some modern dancing ready for the social. We've not got much time now.

Monday 22

We called a meeting at Don's this evening to decide on the programme for the social. I got there early so as to have a game with Linda before the others came. Mother was not too good when she got there – her bronchitis has been bothering her again – but she was O.K. when she had rested for a while. We coped with the whole programme – and of course had a lot of laughs into the bargain.

Tuesday 23

Had my lesson later this evening 7.30! I was too tired really to concentrate.

Wednesday 24

This afternoon I began my class with Betty at the Women's Gas Federation[59]. It was great fun – and it is going to be a terrific help to me. There are about 50 in the class – all raw beginners. I look forward to going again.

Friday 26

We held our dancing in the small hall this evening as we all watched a film from 8.30 to 9 in the large hall. Don has begun his B.B. on Fridays again now, but was back before 10 tonight. He suggested that we go to the Loughton dance tomorrow as they all seemed so keen that I be there.

Saturday 27

Norman took us to the dance, but we came home by tube. It was not very well attended as there were two other dances on quite near – but we had a lovely time. I led off the Veleta/Heather waltz with Harold – Betty introducing me as her deputy! Everyone made us both so welcome and invited us to their dinner in January. On the way home Don said that this was to have been his last dance with me – apart from our own social which he would see me through – when I asked why he said it was a personal matter and did not want to discuss it. I was going to let things go at that, although I was sorry to be losing him. A little later though he told me that in fairness he should tell me that I am so attractive it is impossible for him to see me as a platonic friend, and as I show no interest in him the easiest way is for him to disappear.

---

[59] The Women's Gas Federation was a social club set up in 1953 to promote the domestic use of gas. These sorts of social clubs were not uncommon and would often attract a large crowd.

I was speechless – am I to be jeopardised and lose valued friends through something women envy of me? I could not answer my true feelings – as I still feel nothing should come of our friendship – but decided to have a good talk when we got back to my place. However Mother was up so that put an end to my little talk.

Sunday 28

We took Nan to Eastbourne today! It was grand weather and I should have had a wonderful day, but I kept thinking of how I was going to lose Don and Linda. Also I felt quite guilty – I had been going to his place all alone and leading him on quite unconsciously. What a set up!

Tuesday 30

I had my lesson this evening and told Betty my story – she was not surprised, as she had an idea of his feelings for me. She suggested I let him know my ideas and leave the rest to him.

Figure 35 Iris and Penny, circa 1958.

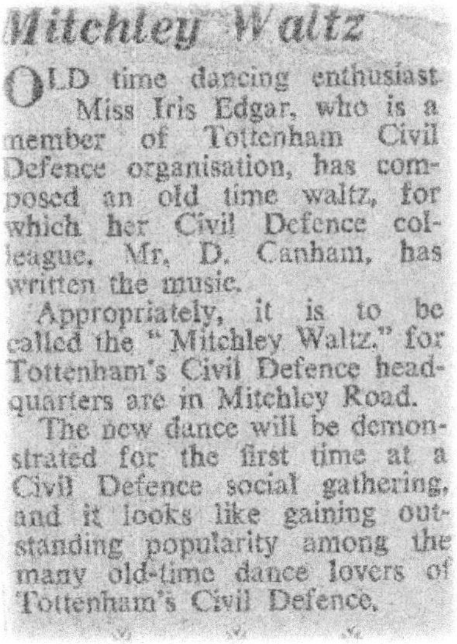

Mitchley Waltz

OLD time dancing enthusiast Miss Iris Edgar, who is a member of Tottenham Civil Defence organisation, has composed an old time waltz, for which her Civil Defence colleague, Mr. D. Canham, has written the music.

Appropriately, it is to be called the "Mitchley Waltz," for Tottenham's Civil Defence headquarters are in Mitchley Road.

The new dance will be demonstrated for the first time at a Civil Defence social gathering, and it looks like gaining outstanding popularity among the many old-time dance lovers of Tottenham's Civil Defence.

Figure 36

October

Rather mild with below average rainfall and sunshine

Wednesday 1

I went to the G. Fed.[60] class again this afternoon – Betty has thought over our problem and her advice is still the same – however she said she doesn't envy my interview with Don this evening.

At Don's we worked hard and arranged the sequence of our programme. I shelved my little talk with him until almost home – I'm a born coward! Then I asked him if he was truly going to disappear after the social, and when he said that he was that he was trying to steel himself against me I explained that I too am steeling myself. His reason is that he couldn't take being hurt again – mine, as I explained, is because I feel I have no right to take on any man particularly one in his circumstances. He said I had never led him on – he just fell in love with me soon after he met me a year ago! Poor devil.

Friday 3

Don seemed much brighter tonight, and we arranged to do our modern dancing tomorrow.

[60] Gas Federation

Saturday 4

Don and Linda came to tea and I went back with them. When Linda went to bed we worked on the Quickstep and Foxtrot. Don put his arm round my shoulders and held my hand at times, when we were checking on our instruction, and somehow I could not help myself letting him. But I wished he would not try my endurance too much. Then we watched T.V. while we had supper. Once T.V. was finished I sat in the armchair and he on the arm once more reading the modern dancing charts when he took my hand and without realising what was happening I was in his arms. All I could say was – "we mustn't". Then I asked him to let me explain my point of view. However he said he would wait for as long as I asked. For the time being I have left it that way. I hope he does wait – for I am in love for the first time in my life. But I am not expecting too much of him. We agreed to see as much of each other as possible – and not to let anyone else know of our love. He won't disappear now – in fact he is going to take dancing seriously – and get an evening suit! It will be great not to have to stifle my feelings any longer.

Sunday 5

There wasn't much I could do today – so I painted all afternoon! But my mind kept wandering back to last evening. I'm longing to tell my Mother but as things cannot take any real shape at the moment I cannot.

Danny was here all day – he is moving this week to Deptford – Norman and Mick are going to miss him.

Monday 6

I think I must have shown my feelings today for Blanche said I look like "the cat that has had the cream".

When I saw Don this evening I wondered how I should feel when face-to-face with him. But I wasn't embarrassed as I thought I should be. We watched the dancing club[61] on T.V. and I didn't get home until late – but I didn't care somehow!

Wednesday 8

Clinic today – I got the best result I have ever had. Don rang to see how I'd fared! He was as pleased as me that I had been given another three months. It's nice having someone apart from Mother and Norman to whom I really matter.

---

[61] According to the 6 October 1958 edition of The Radio Times it was probably Come Dancing that they watched, which was broadcast from the Royal Ballroom, Tottenham. Come Dancing alternated with Victor Sylvester's Dancing Club on Monday nights. Why do I think that my mother and father were not really paying attention to the TV?

Thursday 9

After work this evening I went on up to Don's. We didn't work – just sat and talked.

Friday 10

It was nice working with Don this evening in our new capacity. We were much more of a unit, and I am quite sure we shall make a good job of the social together.

Saturday 11

Don and I went to Bruce Grove Dance Hall[62] this evening to "polish up" our modern dancing. Who should be there with a beau was Mrs. Thompson. She and her partner were "snogging" most of the time. I cannot wait until Monday to tell them at the college! He seems to be much younger than her.

Sunday 12

I met Don today and we walked through to meet Linda from Sunday School, and then went on to his Mother's for tea.

Tuesday 14

My lesson this evening – I feel more confident now.

Wednesday 15

Great fun again this afternoon at the W.G.F. dancing class. We started teaching the Embassy Blues. I think they'll like it when they pick it up properly.

Saturday 18

Pam's wedding! Norman took me down by car, and on the way we called for Dorothy and Mrs. Stone. By doing this it rather broke the ice between us, in fact they seemed as though they couldn't do enough for me. Linda kept by me all the time, but even this didn't seem to bother them. Perhaps if I 'pop-in' to say cheerio when I'm up at Don's I shall be able to keep on some kind of friendly terms with them.

Pam looked lovely, and so did Jean and Linda who were bridesmaids (in blue). Pam and her Mother had made the dresses, and done them well too.

My Mother had made me a cyclamen Nylon dress and grey corduroy velvet coat. She was up most of the night to finish it, but I feel the effort

---

[62] Bruce Grove dance hall was above Bruce Grove cinema and was purpose built by the Tottenham Cinema and Entertainment Co. in 1920.

was worth it.

Don M.C'd the proceedings – and very well too he did it.[63]

Tuesday 21

My lesson was later tonight – not until 8 o'clock.

Wednesday 22

G.B.[64] Meeting this evening – Mr Roe's last one before he retires.

Friday 24

We were having our last dancing class before the social tonight. We went through all the items on the programme – and now I just hope all goes well.

Saturday 25

Dick came this morning. Then I got my things ready for tonight and this afternoon Norman took Mother and I down to Mitchley Road to take sausages etc. Mother stayed down there to prepare refreshments and Norman carried me on to Hursts to do the shopping.

Don came early and we all had a sherry then Norman took us down to the C.D.

The social was a terrific success – Don was a real asset with the games. I hope the other affairs go down as well. After the social we all went back to Miss Rivett's flat for a drink. It was a lovely evening altogether.

Wednesday 29

I got home early this evening from the W.G.F. as I was meeting Don at 7 (and we were meeting Linda from the G.L.B cadets.) It was quite fun doing this.

Friday 31

I had my lesson this afternoon – and found it my easiest to work during the day than in the evening after a day at work.

At the class this evening everyone told us how much they had enjoyed the social. I'm glad it went down so well.

Figure 36 Newspaper cutting, The Mitchley Waltz.

---

[63] In Pam and Gerry's wedding photo my Dad was standing up straight and looking proud between his parents and Pam. St Johns Church where they got married was the church where George Portell and Lillian Lewis married 1923. Their daughter, Lillian Woolmore-Portell, married a US Navy sailor, Barnett Bridges, in London during the Second World War. They then moved to New Orleans and had three children. The youngest, Lynne, married James Spears in 1976. They had three children, the middle one being Britney Spears.

[64] Governing Body – of Middlesex Education Dept. where Iris worked.

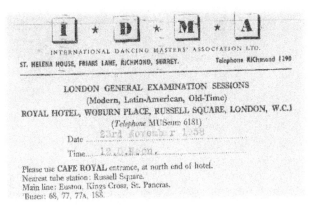

Figure 37

November
Dull and rather dry with near normal temperatures

Saturday 1
I went to see the B.B. six aside football this afternoon – it was cold but good fun. Then went back with Don and Linda to his Mother's for tea.

Sunday 9
Mother and I went over to Olive's to dinner today – Win and her Aunt Glad were also there. We had a lovely time together. The food was not so nice as it usually is at Olive's. We had a lovely time.

Saturday 15
I met Don at the 171 bus stop at 8.30 this morning to start our weekend away at his Aunt's at Waterlooville. We had a wonderful weekend. I slept with Linda, and we laid and talked so much that Don got up and told us off – he thought we should wake Aunt Grace and Uncle Bert up – but they didn't even hear us!

I shall look forward to going there again. We got home late on Sunday night.

Thursday 20
I received my notification of exam this afternoon – my tummy is beginning to get weak already! Then again I am trying to fob my Mother off, so that she doesn't realize when I take my exam.[65]

---

[65] There are three levels of teaching qualification: the first being Associate level. Success at this level would put my mother on the first step towards becoming a professional dance teacher.

Saturday 22

I have developed a horrible cold. This evening I went to Canham's –
Pam and Gerry were there. We sat and drew each other! I couldn't help my
thoughts wandering to tomorrow, and did not get home till well after 12
o'clock, when I was too tired to worry.

Sunday 23

Well, if I pass my exam I shall feel amazed, to say the least! My nerves
were dreadful, and some of the questions were, I'm sure, more than
Associate Grade. Connie Rosslyn, my examiner, was kind and seemed to
allow for nerves – anyway so I hope! She did tell me that I gave a good
performance in my practical. Anyway I shall know on Tuesday.

Tuesday 25

I woke up today, with the thoughts of a 'failed' notice arriving in the
post. However it didn't come! Instead I got a wonderful surprise – I was
commended! A professional at last[66]. Mother was pleased and said she
thought I was trying to pull the wool over her eyes when I told her I was
only partnering medallists on Sunday morning. Betty was thrilled when I
rang her this morning. After all a commended Prof. exam. result is a
"feather in her cap". I broke the news to Don tonight – he was very
pleased, and we celebrated with sherry.

Wednesday 26

Betty told the women at W.G.F. this afternoon that I had gained my
qualification. They all clapped me!

Thursday 27

Presentation of awards! I'm so glad its here at last and perhaps now all
the awful panic of the past few weeks will be finished.

It wasn't a bad 'do', Miss Lane and I presented the bouquets to the
"leading ladies". Mr. Hoffman, the new Principal, was there – and very nice
he seems too!

---

[66] The International Dance Masters Association (IDMA) was formed in Manchester in 1903 as the
Manchester and Salford Association of Teachers of Dancing and went through a series of changes as
dancing grew in popularity.
In 1958 the Birmingham based Midland Dance Teachers' Association changed its name to the Dance
Teachers' Association (DTA). In 1967, the IDMA and DTA merged, becoming the International Dance
Teachers' Association (IDTA) of which my mother was a lifelong member, retaining her maiden name
for her dancing career.

Friday 28

Apparently Mr. Roe was very pleased with the results of the "presentation" last night. I'm glad as it's his last one. Apparently he is very keen on Utrillo's pictures and the G.B. gave him a reproduction for a goodbye present. I'm going to lend him my book on Utrillo[67], as he is so keen.

Don gave me a beautiful bracelet this evening! My present for passing my exam. We arranged for a celebration party at Miss Rivett's place on the 6th Dec.

Figure 38

Frustratingly there is no mention of the recruiting social in the diary. All we have to show its public debut is the above clipping that my father kept.

Figure 37 Notice of IDMA Examination, 1958.
Figure 38 Newspaper cutting, The Mitchley Waltz.

---

[67] Maurice Utrillo was a French painter who died in 1955. He was born in the Montmartre area of Paris and specialised in cityscapes, especially of the area in which he lived. His life was characterised by a bohemian lifestyle, mental illness and alcohol abuse. He lived into his seventies.

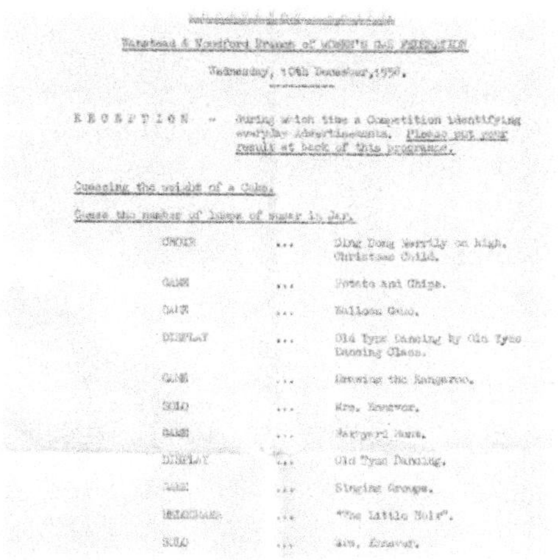

[illegible] Branch of WOMEN'S GAS FEDERATION

Wednesday, 10th December, 1958.

RECEPTION – During which time a Competition identifying everyday Advertisements. Please put your result at back of this programme.

Guessing the weight of a Cake.

Guess the number of lumps of sugar in Jar.

CHOIR	...	Ding Dong Merrily on high. Christmas Child.
GAME	...	Potato and Chips.
GAME	...	Balloon Game.
DISPLAY	...	Old Tyme Dancing by Old Tyme Dancing Class.
GAME	...	Drawing the Kangaroo.
SOLO	...	Mrs. [illegible].
GAME	...	Farmyard Hunt.
DISPLAY	...	Old Tyme Dancing.
GAME	...	Singing Groups.
MELODRAMA	...	"The Little Heir".
SOLO	...	Mrs. [illegible].

Figure 39

December

Dull, wet, and rather mild

Saturday 6

We had a wonderful party this evening. As well as our dancing class Blanche and Lesley and Betty came. Mr. and Mrs. Holland, and the Whites bought me bouquets – I've not had flowers since I was ill! It makes one feel really feminine to be given flowers.

Wednesday 10

Betty and I went to the W.G.F. Xmas party this afternoon[68]. We had a lovely time. I bought Mother a pair of slippers for her birthday.

Saturday 13 and Sunday 14

We went to Pam and Gerry's this weekend. It was interesting to go all round the cattle market – I liked Norwich very much – save that it rained all weekend. There is a funny ghostly atmosphere about Pam's flat[69]. She must

[68] It looks like it was a merry time, from the games like Potato & Chips (no idea) to Farmyard Hunt, the melodrama of "The Little Heir" and of course the old Time Dancing Display by Iris and her dancers. As if that wasn't enough fun the January meeting would see the lucky women of the WGF watch a film show by Unilever and hold a sausage roll cookery competition.

[69] For someone who had a stoic and down to earth attitude to much of her life Mum had an interest and belief in the supernatural. Her mother used to claim that 14 Dorset Road was haunted by a friendly poltergeist that had stopped her being burgled by rattling coat hangers to alert her to someone trying to climb in the window. At other times it was mischievous and hid things like thimbles and needles. The poltergeist was an occasional topic of conversation when we visited her but always in an off-hand way, as if we were just chatting about a naughty kitten.

be dreadfully lonely in it and homesick.

Thursday 25 and Friday 26

I was very late this morning getting up. I'd not been up long when Don and Linda came to show me Linda's 'bike' and thank me for their presents. I bought Linda gold dancing shoes and Don a picture of Vernon Ward's – "Mousehole in Cornwall"[70]. I let Linda come in, but thought it best if Don didn't as I wasn't dressed. After breakfast we opened our presents. I've had the best presents ever.

We spent a very quiet Xmas day, and Boxing Day. Don came round at 10.30 Boxing night and stayed until 1.30. We had decided not to see each other over Xmas, but to spend our time with our families. But after Linda went to bed on Boxing night, he slipped out to see me.

I went to a party at Canham's this evening – we had a lovely silly time.

Sunday 29

Don and Linda came to tea – then I let Linda put my jewellery in the case Don bought me for Xmas. He also bought me a marcasite brooch![71] Then we went back to his place and planned our New Year's Eve party.

Tuesday 31

I met Kate at the clinic this morning. My result was good again. Then this afternoon we at the college had a little tea party given by Mr. and Mrs. Roe, as his farewell to the office staff. It wasn't so bad an ordeal as I had expected!

Our New Year Party was wonderful. We only had a small crowd, but it was a terrific success.

They gave me a bunch of flowers and a huge box of chocolates. Also they gave Mother a bouquet.

I wonder what 1959 holds out for us!

Figure 39 Extract, Woman's Gas Federation Xmas party, 1958.

---

[70] Mousehole Harbour Entrance by Vernon Ward hung on a wall in every house my parents lived in together. It had a strange luminescent quality to it, despite years of grime and neglect. Its last resting place was in the lavatory of their house in Suffolk, and it was one of those things I left for the house clearers after my mother moved into a nursing home. How I wish now that I had known the story behind it then and could have kept it. How foolish I was.

[71] The marcasite brooch is made from pyrite. True mineral marcasite is not used as a gem due to its brittleness. Marcasite used to mean all iron sulphides, which included pyrite and marcasite, and was redefined in 1845, but the older definition remained in the jewellery trade. I'm boring myself now so let us move on…

Figure 40

Chapter 19
And then...1959 – 1984

What 1959 would hold for them was a bit of a mystery but it appears from the evidence available that their love for each other continued to grow. I do know from photograph albums that my parents and Linda went to Skegness during the summer, on holiday I assume.

In 1960 they took Linda on another holiday, this time by train to Oban on the west coast of Scotland. On the journey, as the train passed through Gretna Green, my father proposed.

I've some of the photos from that holiday, Iris and Linda in matching kilt skirts, views from Pulpit Hill over Oban and to the mountains of Mull, landmarks familiar to me now as I live on Mull.

This little stash of photos, uncovered when I found Iris' 1955 and 56 diaries, has brought me closer to my parents, knowing that over 60 years ago they travelled nearly 600 miles to enjoy the same views as I do.

Unlike me though, they went back to London.

They were married on 10 March 1961. They were 35 and 31 years old.

Soon after, they moved into a tidy end of the row house in New Park Avenue in Palmers Green. It was convenient for my father commuting into the city but sufficiently removed to have better air and was a short drive or train ride into the greenbelt surrounding London.

Iris was now an official Instructor and Demonstrator of Old Time Dance and had cards made to this effect. She had her letters after her name. A.I D.M.A. (Comm.) Associate (member of the) International Dancing Masters' Association (Commendation). She kept her maiden name for her professional career her entire life.

Instructor and Demonstrator of Old Time Dancing

IRIS EDGAR, A.1.D.M.A.(COMM.)

97, NEW PARK AVENUE,
PALMERS GREEN 3020.   PALMERS GREEN. N.13.

Figure 41

The house was right next door to a path that led to the park, where doubtless Linda, and later I, would be taken for walks. I came along in April 1963, a little brother to my adoring big sister.

I was too young to remember anything about our time there. The only story I know was the time my mother burnt the kitchen down. According to his account, my father returned from work to find my mother clutching me, standing next to Linda, the dog and the budgie on the doorstep waiting for the fire brigade. Apparently drying cloths above the cooker was not a good idea and this was reinforced with some vigour by the Chief fireman in attendance.

In 1965 the family moved to a new build semi-detached house in Sawbridgeworth, Hertfordshire. BP, who my father still worked for as an accountant, had moved their operations to nearby Harlow, and Sawbridgeworth gave us the opportunity to be snobs and shun the 'London overspill' of new town of Harlow.

An advantage of buying a brand-new house was that my parents could request a wooden floor for the lounge that was to double as mum's dance studio.

One of their first purchases for the new home was a washing line.

By and by my sister's relationship with my parents was to fracture. She left home for pastures new while still a teenager and although they had sporadic contact there was too much hurt for a full and frank reconciliation.

Iris stepped up her dancing as her reputation increased. She taught on

Saturday mornings in the front room, took private lessons for individuals and couples and set up a school of dancing in the church hall.

Saturday evenings began to be reserved for dances, usually with my mother instructing or MC'ing.

I do not recall all the dances I was dragged along to, but I do remember those for the Reliant Owners Club, held in a dingy hall somewhere beginning with B; Braintree or Baldock maybe.

I think it was the embarrassment of having parents who owned a three wheeled fiberglass death trap that made them memorable. I was packed in the back along with boxes of records, the record player and additional speaker, shoe boxes and a holdall of miscellaneous equipment and spares.

My job was to carry the records in and help set up the record player, loudspeaker, and microphone. I would then try to spend the rest of the evening enjoying a sulk in the most inconspicuous spot I could find.

Inevitably I would be propositioned for a dance by ladies who favoured heavy makeup and perfumes from the floral end of the spectrum.

Sometime after the interval, with the raffle for left-over boxes of Christmas chocolates and cans of pilchards[72] completed I would be persuaded to join in, reluctantly at first but eventually I'd be swirling around as if I wasn't a decade or three younger than everyone else present.

My father continued as band instructor with the Boys Brigade in Sawbridgeworth, sometimes taking church parade and Bible classes. His faith was always strong but quiet. He never evangelised and didn't make me attend church.

The Boys Brigade is an unashamedly Christian organisation, and like my father, was Baptist in origin. Their objective is; *"The advancement of Christ's kingdom among Boys and the promotion of habits of Obedience, Reverence, Discipline, Self-respect and all that tends towards a true Christian manliness."*

Maybe I wasn't Christian or manly enough to join, but it never appealed to me.

I do however recall marching beside the band as they paraded around the startled early morning streets of Sawbridgeworth and being particularly impressed at the mace twirling of the band leader upfront. I used to practice in our back garden with an old stick, until the dog ran off with it.

The Boys Brigade motto of *'Sure and Steadfast'* could have been my father's personal motto too.

In 1973 he was successful in his application for a job in Suffolk as an Accountant for The Aldeburgh Festival.

---

[72] On one occasion I 'won' a Yardley soap and a tin of pilchards. I hadn't bought any tickets but as no one claimed them they were presented to me. I'm not sure what they thought a nine-year-old would do with them...as I recall the soap tasted better than the pilchards.

This was a radical move that was influenced by our regular holidays on the East Coast and accelerated when he got wind of looming redundancies at BP.

They purchased a slightly rambling house on the outskirts of Saxmundham, a market town in Suffolk, which sits on the main A12 trunk road halfway between Ipswich and Lowestoft. Somewhat fortuitously; at least for my parents, at the time of purchase the surveyor fell though the floor in one of the front rooms. Consequently, Iris was able to have a brand-new wooden floor installed in what became her dance studio.

It was a short commute to Aldeburgh for my father who by this time had traded three wheels of Reliant embarrassment for four wheels of underpowered Mazda.

It took a while but Saxmundham became home. Iris went from the new woman in town to someone who taught classes for all ages and abilities. Evenings and weekends were peppered with engagements that inevitably involved dancing, as an instructor or MC.

She taught to a high standard and regularly took women and girls (I do not recall any men or boys apart from the very young) for their medal tests, in many cases to IDTA gold medal standard.

She branched out into drama and liturgical (worship) dance in the local church too.

As her reputation grew, she was approached by a social worker who ran an informal social club for adults and young people who had a learning disability. At first it seemed an odd mix. My mother took a no-nonsense approach to dancing and would not accept anything but total commitment and concentration. She wasn't unkind to any of her students, but she certainly didn't pull her punches when it came to correcting one's posture or getting the steps correct.

But it worked.

The members of the club that she taught grew in confidence and ability, to the point where they performed at The Royal Festival Hall, London three times under her tutelage. Some members even took their IDTA medals.

To her enormous credit she never accepted disability, intellectual or physical, as a barrier to anyone achieving success.

My father was ever present, always in the background, doing the practical stuff like ferrying her, the record player and boxes of records around and setting everything up for her.

They had 13 years together in Suffolk, years when I grew up and left home, and Iris got a full-time job working with adults with a learning disability at a local training centre, as it was then called, where she taught dance, drama and art.

She kept up her regular dance classes in the evenings and Saturday mornings and was awarded the IDTA gold lifetime membership.

In 1981 I briefly moved to London as a wide eyed 18-year-old and would call in to see my Nan, Mabel, in Dorset Road. The house smelled of paraffin and damp. There was always (in my memory at least) a tin of pease pudding[73] warming on the top of the dusty pink paraffin heater.

The house never seemed to change.

Norman lived in North London too, where he worked as a bus driver, before relocating to the Isle of Wight, where he drove buses around the island.

Figure 40 Don and Iris, Loughton, 1961.
Figure 41 Iris' Business card.

---

[73] If you have never tried pease pudding, my advice is, don't. Your life is much better without it. It is a savoury dish typically made of boiled split yellow peas. It has the consistency of porridge with none of the exciting taste.

Figure 42

Chapter 20

2020 and all that...

Towards the end of 2020 my wife and I took advantage of a brief window in the Covid-19 lockdown and went back to Tottenham.

Emerging from the Seven Sisters underground station onto the Great North Road we were hit by a cacophony of noise. Car horns, idling buses, revving engines, cycle bells, shouting and conversations in a host of different accents and languages.

With my youngest son, who is now a resident of London himself, we sat outside a coffee shop on the junction of West Green Road and the A10 and let the noise wash over us. It was exhilarating to watch people from different generations, cultures and backgrounds waltzing around, in and out of each other's lives at this anonymous junction at the unglamorous end of North London. To use an old but appropriate cliché, it was a melting pot, just as it had been in the 1950s.

We set off down the West Green Road, past gaudy takeaways, dazzling hairdressers and small supermarkets with shelves packed from floor to ceiling. According to the Royal Society for Public Health, in 2015, out of 146 of London's high streets, West Green Road/Seven Sisters rated as the unhealthiest, based on its impact on the public's health and wellbeing. Muswell Hill, only 3.5 miles away, came out as the healthiest.

Whatever the truth, and their findings have been disputed, the residents of N15 are certainly not short of take-away options.

Under the railway bridge, the commercial street gave way to wider pavements and a variety of houses, flats, and offices.

After Summerhill Road to our right we passed West Green Baptist Church. The same somewhat austere building I knew had bright new signs, a lively notice board and a small cheerful garden, but turning right into

Dorset Road, its wire-grilled windows and walls the colour of dirty sand were just the same as I remember.

Behind the church is Dorset Hall, with its dark recessed doors that gave no clue as to the charms that may be inside. What I thought at first was an estate agent's board turned out to be advertising a nursery. Presumably behind this grim exterior is a world of bright colour and cheerful murals, at least one hopes so for the sake of the local toddler community.

Dorset Road is still a cul-de-sac with cobbles showing where the tarmac has worn away and it retains a feint air of neglect, a road that leads to nowhere except home for its residents.

The cement factory has gone, and new housing stands where it once was. Fortunately, someone in the planning department thought to retain the old walls and gateposts to 'Bysouth Natural Stonework' stonemasons and engraved into them is the legend,

'NO VEHICLES MAY ENTER THESE GATES EXCEPT ON BUSINESS.'

I traced the letters with my finger, these words were there when Iris played in these streets.

Maybe she too traced the letters in an idle moment.

Of course, the focus of our attention was number 14. Surprisingly, it seemed little changed in the 30 or so years since I was last there.

Before we left the area, I had one more place to visit, so we set off before the residents got too suspicious of our presence. Up Philip Lane and left onto Dongola Road, where we paused outside number 90 where my father once lived.

The back streets of this part of Tottenham were quiet and bewitching in their variety until we walked round a bend and downhill to Bruce Grove railway station where the busy A10 splits from Tottenham High Road.

Over the hectic street we re-joined the relative peace of residential Tottenham until we found our objective - Mitchley Road.

The halls are still there, part of the Church of the Good Shepherd. The buildings look well cared for and flowers line the short path to the front doors. I took one and pressed it into my wallet. A little keepsake to remind me of the place my parents met.

Mitchley Road held one last surprise for me. One the wall of the church was a blue plaque with the legend:

'In memory of Ralph Joscelyne.
1899 – 1909
Who was shot on this spot during the Tottenham Outrage on Jan. 23rd 1909
May he rest in peace.
Justorum animae in manu Dei sunt.'[74]

I had never heard of the Tottenham Outrage before. It turns out it was a farcical and tragic affair that, if it were not for the loss of innocent lives, would be comical.

One of the advantages of having someone under 40 with us was that while I was still reading the inscription, my son had looked it up on his phone and could furnish us with the details.

Paul Helfeld and Jacob Lepidus decided to rob the Schnurmann Rubber Factory, by snatching the wages.

It happened that the factory was directly opposite Tottenham Police Station, so a clean getaway was not a likely outcome. Helfeld shot at the chauffeur carrying the money, who escaped injury, and the two made off with the loot. The ensuing chase involved (I kid you not); policemen borrowing guns from the public, commandeered bicycles, a car with a policeman clinging onto its running boards, a tram with 40 policemen on it, a horse and cart, passers-by including duck hunters from the marshes, a football team and local workman, all taking part in the pursuit.

Meanwhile the miscreants took control of a tram and forced the conductor, who had never driven in his life, to drive it, switched to a horse-drawn milk float, which overturned when they took a corner too fast, a grocer's delivery cart, which was painfully slow because they didn't release the brake, and eventually continued on foot.

Separated and cornered both men took their own lives.

During the chase 10-year-old passer-by Ralph Joscelyne and pursuer PC Tyler were both shot and killed, and around twenty other non-fatal casualties were reported.

It was a strange, poignant and comically tragic note to ponder on our way back down Tottenham Highroad and back to the coffee shop where we had met up earlier.

On the way we passed the early 17th Century Tottenham High Cross, which used to mark the centre of Tottenham Village, and over the road, the 18th Century town well. Much of Tottenham has changed since my parent's days, but these two structures would have been familiar landmarks to them, beacons in a rapidly shifting world.

We said goodbye to Tottenham on a wide and windswept street with the sun fading and the last few leaves from the trees of Tottenham Green dancing around us.

It made me think of my Mother's life as one of constant movement. From evacuee and a wartime spent scurrying for shelter, to dancing, always

---

[74] The souls of the righteous are in the hand of God.

dancing. She had little time for nostalgia or looking back, momentum was always forward and if she wasn't teaching a class, she was planning one or preparing a production or worship in church.

Only the TB slowed her down, or at least her body, her mind was still restless. She learnt three languages while confined to bed. Her diary for 1956 held lots of St. Ann's medical records paper, carefully cut in half, with her lists of Italian verbs and French numbers on the back.

Into her world of movement entered my father. A calm and pragmatic man who was happy to be swept up into the dance. Sure and Steadfast to the end.

I picked up a leaf that had blown along the high street to perform a flawless pirouette in front of us, put it in my pocket and went down the steps to the underground train without looking back.

Sometimes you need to keep ahead of the ghosts.

Figure 42 Dorset Road sign, 2020.

Figure 43

Chapter 21
All Change

In 1968 the government announced that the 75,000 strong Civil Defence Corps, together with other volunteer organisations with a Civil Defence role, such as the Industrial Civil Defence Service, Auxiliary Fire Service and the National Hospital Service Reserve, were to be disbanded.

The legacy of the Civil Defence Corps lives on in voluntary services such as Mountain Rescue and the Royal Voluntary Service who carry out a variety of public services and welfare work.

The last Woman's Gas Federation club was formally disbanded in 1993, although a few carried on independently.

Undoubtedly, we live in a more tolerant society in 2020 than 1958. Then the Notting Hill riots focused attention where it was needed, and some changes followed. Public attitudes were more resistant though, and the legacy of Mosley's fascists is still visible in fringe (and some not so fringe) political parties today.

Tottenham was again at the epicentre of racial tensions in 1985 and 2011 when significant demonstrations led to widespread protests and rioting around England.

Once staunchly working class Dorset Road still sits in the 20% of most deprived local authority wards in the country. Unemployment and crime are above average, while access to affordable housing and education standards are significantly lower.

Tony Fisher enjoyed quite a career in dance bands and the studio since he 'approached' Iris in 1958. He played with artists including Ted Heath, Tubby Hayes, John Dankworth, Bert Kaempfert, Frank Sinatra and Ella Fitzgerald. As a session musician he contributed trumpet to Shirley Bassey's 'Big Spender', Tom Jones' 'It's Not Unusual' and 'Delilah', Petula Clark's 'Downtown' and The Beatles' 'Strawberry Fields Forever'.

St Ann's Hospital is now a mixed healthcare campus in South Tottenham in the London Borough of Haringey and is the headquarters for the Barnet, Enfield and Haringey Mental Health NHS Trust.

Most of the factories and heavy industry has disappeared from Tottenham.

Mitchley Road Halls are available to hire – they form part of The Good Shepherd Church in Mitchley Road, in the parish of Saint Mary's Church. It is the home of the 2nd Haringey Boys Brigade Company.

The International Dance Teacher Association (IDTA) is still going strong. According to their website they are:

'…a leading dance qualifications body and membership association for professional dance teachers, with over 6000 members in over 55 countries, we define standards across the widest variety of dance forms, examine performance for both professionals and non-professionals of all ages, develop the skills and professional practice of our members and promote the love of dance across a dynamic, global community.'

T the time of writing Leconfield on the Isle of Wight was still operating as an upmarket Guest House.

The house in Saxmundham was sold in 2014. It has been extensively and sympathetically refurbished by its new owners. My wife and I have a new copy of Mousehole Harbour Entrance by Vernon Ward hanging in our living room.

Pam lives in Stevenage, Hertfordshire. She and Gerry spent many happy years together. Gerry passed away in 2020.

Norman is still living in Ventnor on the Isle of Wright. After years of no contact, we have been corresponding and have talked on the telephone.

Linda is happily married and living on the South coast. In 2016 my wife and I paid her a visit while we were touring around, and it turned out to be an emotional and cathartic experience. We have renewed our ties, been in regular contact and are steadily rebuilding our relationship.

And as for Iris and Don?

Figure 43 Trolly bus at Turnpike Lane, London 1950s.

Figure 44

Chapter 22
1984 - 2018

In 1984 my father retired from full time work with the Aldeburgh Festival. He continued going in part time but became increasingly discontent with work. One day while driving into the office he pulled out to overtake a bin lorry and clipped the side, causing little damage to the car but significant harm to his mental well-being.

He had always been a very safe driver. The sort of person who carried out all the safety checks the car manual tells you to. I don't think he ever broke a speed limit, although to be fair until the 1980s he didn't have a car that could.

He became jittery and anxious after his accident, or perhaps it became more noticeable and had been building for a while. Iris loved him dearly, but she was not the sort of person who could express her feelings or empathise easily.

She was still at work full time and busy many evenings. I was a student at the time, living away, I didn't drive and only spent occasional weekends with my parents.

As he settled after the shake-up of his prang and with the prospect of imminent full retirement looming, he developed a cough. The doctor diagnosed bronchitis and treated him accordingly, and he tried to give up smoking.

His cough persisted, and eventually he received a diagnosis.

In 1986 lung cancer took my father just as he was supposed to be enjoying a well-deserved retirement. Although he had been ill for a while, in the end his death was sudden and unexpected.

He had been a smoker for most of his life, a habit he picked up in the navy. One of my fondest memories of him is watching him smoke a slim cigar while sitting at his desk doing the household accounts or going through some papers for work. To this day the smell of cigar smoke reminds me of him, but with the warm memory comes the cold fact that smoking killed him.

He did not get to see me walk down the aisle, he did not get to see his grandchildren and he did not get to enjoy his retirement, tending to the garden he so loved, after a lifetime of working hard.

If his passing was to set mum back then it was short lived.

She carried on with work and with her classes. She started taking tap dancing lessons and took part in group displays, once again using her gift of dancing for pleasure.

She picked up painting again too, an on-off hobby for all of her life, and my former bedroom in Saxmundhan was converted into her studio. It was always full of half-finished oil paintings. The smell of turpentine and oil paint immediately takes me back there.

In the late 80s Mable ended up moving in with Mum for a while as her health deteriorated and my mother was her carer until Norman found her a care home on the Isle of Wight, close to where he was living.

Mabel passed away in January 1991.

In the following years Iris and Norman became estranged. It had been building for a while but whatever the last straw was, and in truth I don't know, it was final.

The bonds that hold families together can be strong and fragile at the same time. A single rope may hold two ships together and withstand the roughest of conditions, but if the rope is severed both ships will drift apart and may never reunite.

In typical stoic fashion mum carried on.

If she felt hurt, betrayed, guilty or anything else she did not let on. Feelings were always played close to her chest. When my first marriage broke down, I received a note in the post a few weeks later telling me news about her dog, with the coda:

'Sorry to hear about you and (name)'.

We never spoke about why, what went wrong, how I felt or what I was going to do.

That is what I expected. I had been brought up to be independent. It may seem cold, but it was not her problem to solve. I was on my own and would no more ask for help than she would offer it.

As mother son relationships went it was not perfect, but it was perfect for us.

Life went on…she taught her grandchildren to dance until they were old enough to politely refuse, and she carried on with her dancing and teaching. Busier than most people half her age, she continued teaching and dancing well into her 70s.

Eventually time caught up with her.

The tough survivor became increasingly fragile, time and age were beginning to defeat her where TB had tried and failed.

After her fall, when she moved into the care home, I was sorting out some of her belongings to take with her and found a note tucked away. It stopped me in my tracks and made me realise, long before I found her diaries, that the stoic, self-reliant person I had known had a vulnerable side too.

Figure 44 Don and Iris, Sizewell Beach, circa 1985.

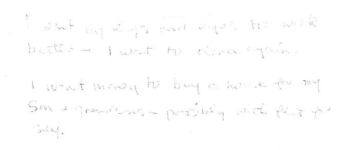

Figure 45

Chapter 23

I want to dance again.

I want my legs and eyes to work better – I want to dance again.
I want money to buy a house for my son & grandsons – possibly with a flat for self.

She was never to dance again.

On the 18th of June 2018 Iris Olive Rose passed away at the James Pagent Hospital in Great Yarmouth, Norfolk.

She had been taken there from the care home a few days earlier and I had been warned that I might not make it in time to see her and say goodbye.

True to form she defied the medical professionals one last time and held on while we raced back from work 500 miles away on the Isle of Mull. Her grandchildren travelled up from the opposite end of the country.

We all got to say goodbye.

And I love you.

We held a funeral for her in the parish church opposite our old house in Saxmundham.

The wake was in the church hall that was such a part of her life, where she danced, choreographed displays, taught toddlers to pensioners, doctors, professors, and adults who had a learning disability, people of mixed ability, disability and gold medal standard partnerships.

She taught them to dance…but more than that she taught them poise, grace, how to express themselves with confidence and to be the best that they could be.

At her funeral some of her former pupils, who were taught by her as young girls, returned as grown women to say goodbye, because after 50 or so years they were still dancing.

Norman did not attend her funeral, but Linda did.

Figure 45 Prayer.

Figure 46

Chapter 24

Reflections

As I write this it occurs to me that until I researched this book, I had always thought of the 1950s as a bleak and monotone place. News footage of the era is usually in black and white, photographs likewise, and somehow my imagination applied its own sepia filter.

Gradually, through reading my mother's diaries London began to take on colour. There was a vibrancy in the dancehalls, the idle gossip and of course in the people. London was changing, a microcosm of the country and of the wider world.

People were recovering from the war, from TB, from smogs (although they weren't gone forever) and new phenomenon, like the teenager, were beginning to establish themselves as a permanent presence.

They were buying the new 45 rpm records in quantities that made marketing people take notice and the business of pop culture started up in earnest. The world was on the cusp of significant change and my parents lived through it, through a World War, serious illness and widowhood, to meet, fall in love and to write their own waltz.

Reading the diaries, I found a woman I knew well yet barely recognised, someone who was familiar yet distant. I saw in that young lady features of the mother I knew, stubborn bloody mindedness, singular ambition, and drive, someone who was confident enough to know that they had a gift and was prepared to put that first.

I found a survivor, somebody who had been through a war, seen her parents get divorced in days when that was uncommon, witnessed goodness knows what in the build up to it, and who had then succumbed to Tuberculosis.

I discovered the tender side of her too, a woman who was torn between career and marriage, who fretted and worried, gossiped and dated, who prayed and danced. Danced for pleasure, for work, for the joy of her gift.

I found the woman who fell in love, despite her misgivings, with a man who was confident yet shy, who already had a daughter, who worked full time, was an officer and instructor with the Boys Brigade and who wrote the melody to accompany the steps she developed.

His role in her story evolved from a walk-on part, when he was volunteered in his absence, to centre stage as leading man. The quiet gentleman who seemed to use Linda to convey his feelings to Iris, and a suspicious (sorry Dad) birthday 'dream' as an excuse to buy Iris chocolates.

But on that train to Scotland Iris Olive Rose Edgar, driven and ambitious, but frustrated by illness, convention and parental responsibilities accepted Donald Alfred Canham's proposal. She persevered, broke the mould, and settled into life away from the suburbs in a way no one, least of all her, expected.

She taught, challenged, and cared in a way that is still remembered with fondness and warmth today.

We may have no record of it now, but the idea of The Mitchley Waltz seems to sum my parents up perfectly; my father adding the melody to my mother's choreography.

Music by Donald Canham.
Steps by Iris Edgar.

Figure 46 Don and Iris, Oban, 1960.

Selected Bibliography

I did a lot of reading for this book, some of it extracts online and some from books and periodicals. I couldn't possibly list everything that I dipped into on here because it would be too long and anyway that assumes that I remember them all, which I don't.

Below are some of the primary sources that I used and returned to. If you think that I haven't got the formatting of my references correct, you obviously care about it more than I do.

A Brief History of Civil Defence, *Civil Defence Association* -Tim Essex-Lopresto.

Lonnie Donegan and the Birth of British Rock & Roll, *The Robson Press* - Patrick Humphries.

Not Always One and the Same Thing: The Registration of Tuberculosis Deaths in Britain, 1900–1950, *Social History of Medicine, Volume 9, Issue 2* - Linda Bryder.

Going to the Palais: A Social and Cultural History of Dancing and Dance Halls in Britain, 1918-1960 *Oxford University Press* - James Nott

Policy Papers in Ethnic Relations No.11 - Centre for Research in October 1987, *University of Warwick* - Bob Carter, Clive Harris & Shirley Joshi.

The History of Live Music in Britain, Volume I: 1950-1967: From Dance Hall to the 100 Club, *Routledge* - Simon Frith, Matt Brennan, Martin Cloonan, Emma Webster

Swingtime in Tottenham, *Lemon Tree Press* - Benny Green

Tuberculosis Sanatorium Regimen in the 1940s: a patient's personal diary – *Journal of the Royal Society of Medicine Volume 97* - Raymond Hurt.

Mass Media, Popular Culture and Social Change in Britain since 1945, *Edexcel* - Stuart Clayton,

Changing Role and Status of Women during the 20th Century, *Aberystwyth* - Colin P. F. Hughes, Catrin Stevens and R. Paul Evans.

harringayonline.com
london-weather.eu
british-history.ac.uk
academic.oup.com
unionhistory.info
cambridge.org
mixmag.net
haringey.gov.uk
rsph.org.uk

About the Author

Born in London and raised in Hertfordshire and Suffolk, Ray was drifting through high school until he discovered punk rock. From then on, he spent his time nurturing a singular lack of musical ability, until realising too late that exam success might have been a better option. Despite his abysmal school results, he went on to forge a career as a nurse, such was the desperation of the NHS in the early 80s.

In 2016 he and his wife Alison decided to leave the rat race, so they sold their home and spent the year living in a motorhome.

Life on the road re-ignited a desire to write that had never been entirely extinguished despite the best efforts of his teachers. His previous writing experience includes company annual reports, a punk rock fanzine and forging notes from his mother to excuse him from PE.

In 2018 he published his first book, **Downwardly Mobile**, documenting his and Alison's life on the road and spending the best part of 2016 working at festivals and discovering the UK from the vantage point of their Motorhome called Mavis.

'A great read! The sense of humour of the author is evident throughout…If you've ever wondered why you live like you do and feel like you have the potential to swap the rat race for a more relaxing way of life you may well find this book inspiring.'

'I found it a real pleasure and joy to read … and it isn't just any old travel adventure book, either. There's history, there's humour, there's behind the scenes at music festivals and you also get the laugh-out-loud family reminiscences as a side dish!'

'You could imagine yourself looking out of the window and seeing it with your own eyes, such was the way it was described. Be prepared to laugh out loud, I got some funny looks when reading this on the bus when I would chuckle and then cry in equal measure. Be sure to read this book.'

———

After moving to the Isle of Mull and living in their motorhome while working at a 14th century castle, Ray published the next instalment of his and Alison's adventures in **Still Following Rainbows**. It documents the highs and lows of adjusting to life and work on Mull, with snippets of history, vivid descriptions of the landscape and plenty of humour.

"I absolutely loved this. It was so well written, and the brilliant descriptions made me feel part of Alison and Ray's journey. Many parts made me laugh out loud and others made me feel quite emotional."

"I want to visit this beautiful island when we are next in Scotland. It sounds amazing and Rays' descriptions of the scenery was so good, I felt I was there!"

"I cannot recommend this book highly enough. Ray is a gifted storyteller, and his words have the power to draw out a whole range of emotions as we journey with himself, Alison, and Mavis to a new life on a Scottish island. It's real, it's raw and it will make you want to visit Mull!"

———

At the beginning of the lockdown in 2020 Ray decided to do his bit for the Covid-19 lockdown and raid his scrap book for unpublished articles, short stories and pieces cut from his other books as an economy-priced diversion for everyone stuck at home. So, he published **Even Unicorns Die** - a collection of short stories, articles and assorted nonsense.

"Wow! This is very different from Ray's autobiographical writing: be warned! It's a delight to read - but don't let that fool you into expectations of a collection of lightweight, heart-warming, feel-good fuzz. This writing has depth and darkness. There are political observations, stories with unexpected stings, thought-provoking reflections, hellish humour, and an alphabet rhyme which you wouldn't want anywhere near your children! It's good. Very good! Order a copy at once!"

"I loved this collection of short stories and articles. A page-turner as you never know quite what Ray is going to write next! The dark verse was a real surprise. Great read and would thoroughly recommend."

"Provocative, punchy punk-fiction. I say fiction, but I get a sense it straddles real life for the author in many places. Sometimes scathing, other times scintillating. This hotchpotch of short stories and observations is well worth your time and, let's be honest, very little of your money."

Coming Next!

Look out for the third instalment of Ray and Alison's adventures as they face the 2020 Covid pandemic and lockdown in a remote 14th century Scottish castle.

Provisionally titled **Duart in Lockdown,** all proceeds will be going towards the castle restoration, a major project that relies upon income from visitors, who have been significantly lower in number than usual because of the pandemic and restrictions on the business.

If you'd like to be informed when it is published or have any other questions or queries you can contact the author at rayscanham@gmail.com.

Thank you for persevering to the end.

Ray

April 2021

Printed in Great Britain
by Amazon